The Resilient Mind

Harnessing Inner Strength to Guide the Body

Dr. C. A. Castillo

Dr. C. A. Castillo

DEDICATION

To my children, Malique, Cammron, and Chalize, you are my inspiration, my motivation, and my living legacy. Watching you grow into strong, intelligent, and compassionate individuals fuels my purpose. May you always draw from your inner strength and resilience as you chase your dreams.

To Elizabeth Castillo, the woman who blessed me with my children. Thank you so much for being a blessing and adding to my blessings. To my parents, family, and ancestors, your sacrifices built the foundation on which I now stand. The values you instilled in me, which included perseverance, discipline, and faith, continue to guide and shape my path.

To my brothers and sisters in arms, your courage, resilience, and unwavering dedication have left an indelible mark on my life. This book honors the strength we share, the burdens we carry, and the healing we seek.

To my clients and to all who are on a journey of self-discovery and healing, may this book offer guidance, hope, and a reminder that even in our darkest battles, the mind remains our most powerful ally. Strength is not the absence of struggle but the choice to rise through it.

With deep gratitude and unwavering purpose.

Dr. C. A. Castillo

FOREWORD

Resilience is not just a concept; it is a necessity for survival, growth, and success. Life presents us with challenges, setbacks, and adversities, but the way we respond to these obstacles defines the trajectory of our lives. The Resilient Mind: Harnessing Inner Strength to Guide the Body is a powerful testament to the human ability to adapt, overcome, and thrive, even in the face of hardship.

As a retired Army officer, a mental health clinician, and a dedicated life coach, Dr. C. A. Castillo has spent decades studying the mind and its profound influence over the body. His journey, from his early years in Dangriga, Belize, to serving in the military and guiding countless individuals through their struggles, has given him firsthand insight into the power of resilience. His experience is not just theoretical; it is lived, tested, and refined through personal and professional challenges.

In this book, Dr. Castillo explores the intricate connection between the mind and body, offering practical strategies to develop mental toughness, emotional stability, and unwavering inner strength. Through research-backed insights, real-life examples, and his own experiences, he provides a roadmap for those seeking to regain control of their thoughts, emotions, and overall well-being. Whether you are navigating personal hardships, professional obstacles, or emotional turmoil, the lessons within these pages will empower you to rise above limitations and grow a resilient mindset.

Resilience is not about avoiding pain; it is about facing it, learning from it, and emerging stronger. This book is an invitation to embark on that journey, to embrace the challenges ahead with confidence, and to discover the immense power that lies within your mind.

Dr. Castillo has dedicated his life to helping others transform adversity into strength. Now, through The Resilient Mind, he shares his knowledge, wisdom, and passion with the world. I invite you to turn the page and begin this transformative journey.

Peter J. Martinez

Business owner of Magicallmoment, mentor, and Brother

CONTENTS

Acknowledgments

First and foremost, I want to express my deepest gratitude to my family, my children, Malique, Cammron, and Chalize, who have been my greatest inspiration and driving force behind this book. Their unwavering love and support continue to motivate me to strive for excellence in everything I do.

To my wife, whose patience and belief in me have carried me through the most challenging moments; your strength and love are the foundation of my success.

I would also like to extend my thanks to the mentors and colleagues who have shaped my professional journey. Your guidance, knowledge, and wisdom have been invaluable.

A special thank you goes to ChatGPT for assisting me in the writing process. The conversations, ideas, and insights generated through this powerful tool have played an essential role in bringing my vision for this book to life. Your support in shaping ideas, refining thoughts, and organizing content has been instrumental in the development of this work.

To my readers, I hope the lessons and insights shared within these pages help guide you toward greater resilience and a deeper understanding of your inner strength. Please remember that although I am a clinician, I am not your clinician. Please seek help from a professional if necessary.

Finally, I am deeply grateful to all those who have contributed, directly or indirectly, to the success of this book. Your support means more than words can express. My brother Peter Martinez was there for me throughout this process. Thank you very much for always being my sounding board.

Preface

Resilience is more than just a trait; it is a skill, a mindset, and a way of life. Throughout my journey as a soldier, a mental health clinician, and a life coach, I have witnessed firsthand how the mind shapes our ability to endure, adapt, and overcome. The ability to harness mental strength is not reserved for a select few; it is within all of us, waiting to be developed and refined. This book is a guide to understanding and unlocking that power.

The inspiration for The Resilient Mind stems from my own experiences and the countless individuals I have worked with over the years. From the battlefield to the therapy room, I have seen the effects of trauma, stress, and adversity, and, more importantly, I have seen the incredible transformations that occur when people take control of their thoughts, emotions, and responses. Resilience is not about avoiding struggle but about facing it head-on with the knowledge that we can emerge stronger on the other side.

The Cover: A Symbol of Strength and Healing

The cover of this book is more than just an image; it is a powerful representation of resilience, healing, and transformation. At its center is the phoenix, the legendary bird that rises from its ashes, symbolizing renewal and unwavering strength. The phoenix embodies the essence of resilience, the ability to withstand adversity, to rebuild, and to soar once more.

However, this phoenix carries a more profound message. A tear falls from its eye, representing healing. True resilience is not just about enduring hardship but also about acknowledging pain, allowing oneself to heal, and emerging stronger. The tears flow downward, forming a turquoise body of water, symbolizing renewal, hope, and emotional restoration.

Beneath the surface of this water lies a brain, submerged yet waiting to rise. The brain represents the mind, our thoughts, emotions, and cognitive strength. As the phoenix's healing tears form the water, they lift the brain from beneath, signifying the transformative power of resilience. When we embrace healing, we unlock the true potential of our minds, gaining clarity, strength, and control over our lives.

This visual is the essence of The Resilient Mind. The phoenix represents resilience, the tear represents healing, and the brain represents the mind, each interconnected, each essential for growth. This book will guide you through the process of strengthening your mind, embracing healing, and ultimately rising above life's challenges with newfound power.

The character in this book named Dominique was chosen because it means Belonging to God. Dominique is a unisex name, and there are many of them. Dominique always felt unwanted; however, over time, she realized that she was always wanted. God wanted her. From her conception to where she is now, He has protected, cared for, and loved her even when she did not realize it.

The Journey Ahead

In these pages, I explore the profound connection between the mind and body, providing research-backed strategies and real-life examples to help you develop mental toughness. This book is for anyone seeking to break free from self-doubt, navigate life's obstacles, and build a foundation of lasting resilience. Whether you are a professional striving for excellence, a service member overcoming hardship, or someone simply looking for ways to manage stress more effectively, the principles outlined here will provide you with the tools to thrive.

I hope that this book serves as both a guide and a source of encouragement. Developing a resilient mind is not a one-time achievement; it is a lifelong journey. By choosing to strengthen your mind, you take control of your body, your emotions, and your destiny.

Thank you for allowing me to be part of your journey. May these pages inspire you to harness the strength within and move forward with confidence, purpose, and resilience.

Dr. C. A. Castillo

Introduction

"To understand the mind is to unlock the map to your soul. This is not therapy. This is truth, reflection, and reclaiming power."

-Dr. C. A. Castillo

The Power of the Mind

The human mind is the most powerful tool we possess. It serves as the command center of our thoughts, emotions, and actions, shaping the way we experience the world. Our minds can propel us toward greatness or trap us in cycles of self-doubt and fear.

When harnessed effectively, the mind has the power to overcome adversity, foster resilience, and guide the body toward healing and strength. But if left unguarded, persistent negative thinking, chronic stress, and emotional turmoil can manifest physically, leading to exhaustion and even illness. Understanding the deep connection between the mind and body is essential to achieving true well-being.

Resilience isn't merely an innate trait; it's a skill that can be developed. Throughout history, countless individuals have demonstrated extraordinary mental strength in the face of immense hardship. From athletes pushing past physical limits to survivors rebuilding their lives after trauma, their ability to endure stems from the mind's capacity to adapt, reframe, and persevere. Scientific research supports this: our thoughts influence physiological responses affecting heart rate, immune function, pain tolerance, and recovery. By training the mind, we can enhance our ability to navigate life's challenges with greater ease and confidence.

But mental resilience isn't only for moments of crisis; it shapes our daily lives. It influences how we manage stress, nurture relationships, and maintain a sense of direction and purpose. Like any skill, it requires consistent, intentional practice.

1

Building resilience means developing self-awareness, practicing optimism, and incorporating mindfulness into our routines. Just as the body grows stronger through physical training, the mind gains strength when we challenge unhelpful thought patterns and develop healthier coping strategies.

In a world defined by rapid change and uncertainty, learning to harness the power of the mind is more important than ever. Whether we're facing personal setbacks, professional stressors, or unforeseen life events, resilience becomes the anchor that grounds us. It doesn't eliminate adversity, but it changes how we respond to it.

This book offers practical tools and evidence-based strategies for building mental toughness. You'll learn to control your thoughts and emotions and ultimately reclaim agency over your life. The journey toward a resilient mind begins with a single step: the belief in the power that already lies within you.

By mastering the mind-body connection, you can unlock your full potential and move through life with clarity, confidence, and strength. Resilience isn't just about surviving hardship. It's about evolving through it, thriving, growing, and using the power of the mind to lead the body toward a purposeful, fulfilling life.

The Role of the Mind in Navigating Life

Understanding the power of the mind is only the beginning; the next step is learning how to apply this power in everyday life. Life presents an endless series of challenges. Some challenges may be predictable, while others are unexpected. Our ability to navigate these challenges depends on how we train our minds.

Just as a well-conditioned athlete performs under pressure, a resilient mind remains steady amidst uncertainty, guiding us toward solutions rather than surrendering to obstacles. The way we perceive and interpret life's difficulties ultimately shapes our ability to move forward with confidence and clarity. The mind serves as both a filter and a compass, influencing how we interpret our experiences and the decisions we make.

When we develop resilience, we shift our perspective from seeing setbacks as failures to viewing them as opportunities for growth. This mental shift is crucial, as it determines whether we remain stuck in frustration or push forward with determination. Those who master their minds are better able to regulate their emotions, make sound decisions, and maintain a sense of control, even in the face of adversity.

Emotional intelligence plays a key role in this process. A resilient mind does not ignore emotions but instead acknowledges and channels them productively. Fear, doubt, and frustration are natural responses to difficulty, but they do not have to dictate our actions. By developing emotional awareness and practicing mindfulness, we can learn to respond to life's challenges with composure and adaptability rather than reacting impulsively or with despair. Strengthening the mind means finding a balance between emotional awareness and rational decision-making.

Furthermore, the way we train our minds influences our relationships and interactions with others. A strong, resilient mind fosters empathy, patience, and effective communication, which are essential qualities for enhancing both personal and professional relationships. When we develop mental discipline, we become more intentional in our words and actions. This can help reduce unnecessary conflict and enhance our ability to connect with others. Whether in leadership roles, partnerships, or social interactions, the mind's ability to regulate thoughts and emotions directly impacts the quality of our relationships.

Ultimately, navigating life successfully requires more than intelligence or physical endurance. It demands mental resilience. By sharpening our awareness, enhancing emotional strength, and maintaining a growth mindset, we can prepare ourselves to handle the inevitable ups and downs of life. The mind is not just a tool for survival; it is the foundation for fulfilling our purpose-driven existence. When we take charge of our thoughts, we take charge of our destiny, paving the way for a life defined not by circumstances but by the strength of our inner resolve.

A Clinician's Perspective on Mental Resilience

Understanding how the mind navigates life's challenges naturally leads to a deeper exploration of how we strengthen it. While many approaches to mental resilience come from therapeutic or counseling frameworks, this book offers a different perspective. It is rooted in the practical insights of a mental health clinician.

Rather than focusing solely on diagnosing or treating mental health conditions, this perspective emphasizes proactive strategies for building mental strength, personal growth, and self-mastery. The goal is not just to manage difficulties but to develop a resilient mindset that enables individuals to thrive in all aspects of life. The distinction between a clinician and a therapist or counselor is essential.

A therapist primarily works with individuals to address mental health challenges through structured interventions. At the same time, a clinician takes a broader approach, analyzing patterns of thought, behavior, and resilience in diverse populations. This perspective allows for a more comprehensive understanding of how mental resilience applies to various life domains, including personal, professional, and social. By drawing from research, real-world observations, and practical applications, this book seeks to provide a holistic approach to mental strength.

Resilience is not just a concept to be discussed in therapy sessions; it is a necessary skill for navigating everyday life. Whether facing stress at work, personal setbacks, or unforeseen crises, individuals must rely on their mental toughness to adapt and persevere. As a clinician, my focus is on equipping individuals with tools that extend beyond traditional therapy, fostering a proactive mindset that strengthens mental endurance in real-world situations. Mental resilience is not just about overcoming trauma or hardship; it is about consistently building inner strength, self-awareness, and the ability to regulate emotions in any circumstance.

This perspective also acknowledges that mental resilience is a profoundly personal journey. No two individuals experience life in the same way, and what works for one person may not work for another. A clinician's approach embraces this individuality, offering adaptable techniques rather than rigid prescriptions. This book provides a framework for mental resilience that readers can personalize, drawing from science, personal reflection, and lived experiences. The goal is to empower individuals to take control of their mental well-being without relying solely on external guidance.

By writing from a clinician's perspective, this book aims to bridge the gap between theory and practical application. It is not a guide to therapy, nor is it a clinical manual. It is a roadmap to understanding and harnessing the power of the mind for lasting resilience. As you move forward, you will discover evidence-based strategies, real-life examples, and actionable steps designed to strengthen mental endurance. This journey is about more than knowledge. It is about transformation, self-discovery, and unlocking the full potential of a resilient mind.

Becoming One with the Mind

Understanding mental resilience from a clinician's perspective provides valuable insights into strengthening the mind, but true mastery requires something more profound: becoming one with the mind itself. Resilience is not merely about reacting to challenges; it is about developing an intimate connection with our thoughts, emotions, and inner dialogue. When we achieve this level of awareness, we gain the ability to shape our responses, direct our energy, and create a mindset that promotes growth rather than resistance. Mental resilience is not just a tool; it is a state of being.

Too often, individuals see their minds as separate from their experiences, treating thoughts and emotions as forces beyond their control. However, true mental strength comes from recognizing that we are not victims of our minds but active participants in shaping them. Becoming one with the mind means understanding how it functions, acknowledging its patterns, and learning to guide it with intention. This requires self-awareness, mindfulness, and the willingness to challenge limiting beliefs that keep us trapped in cycles of doubt and negativity.

Achieving harmony with the mind does not mean eliminating struggle or silencing difficult emotions. Instead, it involves learning how to coexist with discomfort while maintaining clarity and focus. Life will always present uncertainties and obstacles, but a mind that is trained to adapt rather than resist remains steady in the face of adversity. This is the foundation of true resilience, embracing challenges as opportunities to deepen our understanding of ourselves rather than as threats to our stability.

Developing this connection with the mind is a process that requires patience and practice. It is created through intentional reflection, disciplined thought patterns, and mindfulness techniques that allow us to observe our mental processes without being controlled by them. When we become one with the mind, we unlock a new level of personal power, one that enables us to navigate life with greater confidence, emotional balance, and purpose. The mind is not our enemy; it is our greatest ally when we learn to work with it rather than against it. The mind can be both our best friend and our worst enemy.

As we explore what it means to become one with the mind, this book will offer practical strategies to help you strengthen this connection. From mindfulness exercises to cognitive reframing techniques, you will discover tools that encourage a deeper understanding of your mental landscape. The journey to mastering the mind is not about forcing control but about fostering alignment. An alignment that allows resilience to flow naturally and effortlessly in every aspect of life.

The Mind's Role in Controlling the Body

Becoming one with the mind is a crucial step toward resilience, but true mastery extends beyond mental awareness. It involves understanding the profound connection between the mind and the body. The way we think, feel, and process emotions directly influences our physical state, shaping everything from our energy levels to our overall health. The mind is not just a source of thoughts; it is the command center that regulates the body's responses, proving that mental strength and physical well-being are inseparable.

Science has long demonstrated the impact of mental processes on bodily functions. Stress, anxiety, and negative thinking can manifest physically, leading to fatigue, high blood pressure, and even chronic illness. Conversely, a calm, focused, and resilient mind can enhance immune function, improve recovery, and increase overall vitality. The way we perceive challenges and respond to stress determines whether our bodies remain in a state of tension or relaxation. This intricate relationship highlights the importance of mental discipline in maintaining physical health.

One of the most potent examples of the mind's control over the body is seen in athletes, military personnel, and individuals who push their physical limits. These individuals rely not just on physical conditioning but on mental resilience to endure pain, exhaustion, and setbacks. Their ability to harness the mind's power allows them to break barriers that might otherwise seem impossible. This same principle applies to everyday life. Whether overcoming illness, managing pain, or simply maintaining energy and motivation, the mind plays a decisive role in determining physical outcomes.

Moreover, the body often mirrors the state of the mind. A person burdened by stress may experience muscle tension, headaches, or digestive issues, while someone with a balanced mindset often exhibits greater physical ease and relaxation. This mind-body connection reveals that true well-being requires more than exercise or proper nutrition; it demands mental clarity, emotional regulation, and a deep understanding of how thoughts influence the body's responses. Recognizing this link empowers individuals to take proactive steps in both mental and physical self-care.

As we explore the mind's role in controlling the body, this book will delve into practical strategies to align mental and physical well-being. From breathing techniques that regulate stress responses to cognitive practices that enhance endurance and pain management, understanding this connection allows us to take control of our overall health. The mind is not just a tool for thinking. It is the key to unlocking physical strength, healing, and resilience. Learning to harness this power is the next step in achieving a balanced and resilient life.

Introducing Dominique: The Story Within the Story

Understanding the mind's power, its role in navigating life, and its connection to the body sets the stage for a deeper exploration, one that is best illustrated through lived experience. To bring these concepts to life, this book introduces Dominique, a woman whose journey embodies the principles of mental resilience. Dominique's story is not just an example; it is a reflection of the struggles, triumphs, and transformations that many experience. Through her narrative, readers will witness the mind's ability to endure hardship, shape perception, and ultimately guide the body toward healing and strength.

Dominique's journey seamlessly connects to each section of this introduction. She begins as someone unaware of the true power of her mind, struggling with self-doubt and emotional turmoil. As she learns to navigate life's challenges, she gradually discovers the importance of becoming one with her mind, learning to control her thoughts rather than being controlled by them. Her experiences further highlight the profound impact of the mind on the body, illustrating how stress, resilience, and mental discipline manifest physical well-being. Through her story, the theoretical concepts discussed earlier become tangible, offering a personal perspective that deepens the reader's understanding.

By following Dominique's journey throughout this book, readers will not only gain insight into the principles of mental resilience but also see how these lessons apply in real-world situations. Her struggles and breakthroughs serve as a guide, reinforcing the themes of self-mastery, adaptability, and inner strength. As we transition into her story, we move beyond theory and into the lived reality of resilience, where the mind's strength is tested, refined, and ultimately harnessed to guide both the self and the body toward growth and transformation.

Overview of the Journey Ahead

This book is designed to take you on a transformative journey, exploring the intricate relationship between the mind and resilience. Through Dominique's story and evidence-based strategies, each chapter builds upon the last, providing you with the knowledge and tools needed to harness the power of your mind. From understanding the mind-body connection to developing grit, managing emotions, and applying coping strategies, this book serves as a guide to building a resilient mindset.

Chapter 1: The Mind-Body Connection

The foundation of resilience begins with recognizing the profound connection between the mind and the body. This chapter explores how thoughts and emotions influence physical well-being and how stress, trauma, and mental resilience manifest in the body. It delves into scientific research on neuroplasticity, the response to stress, and the role of mindfulness in bridging the gap between mental and physical health. Understanding this relationship is the first step toward harnessing the power of the mind to guide the body.

Chapter 2: Well-Being, Grit, and Resilience

Building resilience requires more than mental strength; it involves building overall well-being and grit. This chapter defines resilience beyond simply bouncing back from adversity; it is about thriving despite challenges. Readers will learn about the role of perseverance, adaptability, and self-care in fostering well-being. Through real-life examples and research-backed insights, this chapter provides a framework for strengthening resilience in everyday life.

Chapter 3: Navigating Negative Emotions

Negative emotions are an inevitable part of life, but how we respond to them determines our resilience. This chapter examines the science behind emotions such as fear, anger, and sadness, offering strategies to acknowledge, process, and regulate them effectively. Rather than avoiding difficult emotions, readers will learn how to use them as tools for self-discovery and growth.

Chapter 4: The Power of Positive Emotions

While negative emotions demand attention, positive emotions serve as a powerful counterbalance. This chapter highlights the role of gratitude, hope, love, and joy in building mental strength. It explores how growing positive emotions enhance resilience and well-being, providing readers with practical ways to shift their mindset toward a more optimistic and empowered outlook.

Chapter 5: Tools for Coping with Emotions

Resilience is built through intentional action. This chapter introduces evidence-based coping mechanisms for managing emotions, including mindfulness, cognitive restructuring, and stress-reduction techniques. Readers will gain practical exercises designed to increase self-awareness and emotional regulation, providing a strong foundation for mental resilience.

Chapter 6: Additional Tools for Coping with Emotions

Building upon the previous chapter, this section delves deeper into advanced coping strategies, including visualization techniques, grounding exercises, and self-compassion practices. It emphasizes the importance of a personalized approach to resilience, encouraging readers to explore different tools and discover what works best for them.

Chapter 7: Dominique's Use of Tools for Healing

Bringing theory into practice, this chapter revisits Dominique's story, illustrating how she applies the coping strategies introduced in earlier chapters. Readers will witness her struggles, setbacks, and triumphs, seeing firsthand how resilience is developed through consistent practice. Dominique's journey serves as a relatable and inspiring example, reinforcing the importance of perseverance and self-compassion in healing.

Chapter 8: Lessons from the Journey

Reflection is a crucial aspect of resilience. This chapter synthesizes the key takeaways from Dominique's story and the strategies introduced throughout the book. Readers are encouraged to reflect on their own experiences, identifying patterns and insights that will support their growth moving forward. This chapter serves as a bridge to the final step of the journey, actively applying these lessons in daily life.

Chapter 9: Journey to Healing: A Path to Resilience

Healing is an essential part of resilience. It emphasizes the ongoing nature of personal growth, encouraging readers to continue practicing the tools and techniques introduced in the book. With Dominique's story as a guiding example, this chapter offers motivation and direction for embracing resilience as a lifelong journey. Readers will leave with a renewed sense of empowerment, ready to take control of their mental well-being and use the power of their minds to guide their body and their lives.

Chapter 10: Building a Stronger You: Words, Strategy, and Action

The final chapter provides a roadmap for long-term resilience. As we close the introduction to this journey, remember that the mind is more than just a processor of thoughts; it is the engine behind every action, every reaction, and every sensation we experience. Before we can fully develop resilience, we must first understand the powerful and often overlooked connection between the mind and the body. In the next chapter, we'll dive into the science and lived truth behind this relationship, exploring how our thoughts shape our health, our posture mirrors our emotions, and our inner world creates the lens through which we see the outer one. This connection is not only real; it's foundational.

Chapter 1
Mind-Body Connection

*"I learned in uniform what my ancestors already knew; resilience is not taught;
it is remembered in the bones."*

-Dr. C. A. Castillo

The heart may be the most vital organ in sustaining life, but the mind
is the most potent force we possess. This chapter invites you to
explore that idea through a series of thought-provoking questions.
For instance, when a person is brain-dead and on life support, are
they genuinely living or simply alive?

Let's take a step back.

Breathing is something we do automatically, without conscious
effort. But what if that process stopped? Of course, we know what
will happen, and life will end. While the question may be rhetorical,
the answer points to something profound: the mind is central to even
our most basic life functions, like breathing.

Yet, many people go through life unaware of how their minds
work or the immense power they hold. The brain, much like a
computer, processes billions of bits of information every second.
Different regions of the brain govern different functions: emotion,
memory, decision-making, and movement. When these parts work
together, they can transform how we live, think, and heal.

As a mental health professional, I've seen firsthand how
understanding the mind can bring profound change. This book is my
way of paying homage to the mind and its untapped potential. I hope
that by the end of these pages, you will develop a deeper bond with
your mind, one that nurtures self-awareness, emotional strength, and
resilience.

When you begin to understand how your mind operates its
thoughts, impulses, strengths, and even fears, you start to unlock a
powerful truth: your body often responds to the commands of your

mind. Learning how to work with your mind rather than against it can be life-changing.

This book also provides practical tools to help you harness this mind-body connection, especially in times of emotional challenge or stress. If even one reader walks away with a new ability to calm their body by understanding their mind, then this writing has served its purpose. The relationship between the mind and body is deeply intricate. But understanding this connection of how thoughts influence physical responses and how physical states shape mental ones is essential to healing, growth, and overall well-being.

The Brain

According to the Oxford Dictionary, the brain is "an organ of soft tissue contained in the skull of vertebrates, functioning as the coordinating center of sensation and intellectual and nervous activity."

The brain is often described as the most complex organ in the human body, and for good reason. It serves as the control center for nearly every bodily function, from basic motor skills to higher-level thinking and emotional processing. Weighing approximately three pounds, the brain is composed of billions of neurons that transmit messages throughout the body via chemical and electrical signals.

One of the brain's most remarkable qualities is its ability to adapt. This adaptability is due to what scientists call neuroplasticity, the brain's capacity to change its structure and function in response to learning, experience, or injury. Through this plasticity, the brain learns new skills, strengthens memory, and even recovers from trauma.

This recovery potential allows the brain to develop continuously, especially in areas like skill acquisition, emotional regulation, and cognitive resilience. However, despite its incredible strengths, the brain is also vulnerable. It can be affected by a range of neurocognitive disorders, such as dementia and Alzheimer's disease. For this reason, maintaining brain health is essential. Habits such as proper nutrition, regular physical activity, mental stimulation, and effective stress management play a critical role in supporting brain function and overall well-being.

Facts About the Brain

The human brain is an incredibly complex and fascinating organ. While we won't dive into every intricate detail here, there are a few essential facts worth remembering for this book. In addition to what's already been shared, it's helpful to understand the roles of serotonin, dopamine, and neurotransmitters, chemical messengers that significantly influence mood, behavior, and bodily functions.

Interestingly, about 70–80% of the brain consists of liquid, which aligns with the fact that the human body itself is approximately 70% water. The average brain weighs around three pounds and is composed of four main lobes: the frontal lobe, parietal lobe, temporal lobe, and occipital lobe. Of these, the frontal lobe is the last to develop fully and plays a critical role in decision-making, emotional regulation, and higher-level thinking.

There's a common myth that humans only use 10% of their brains. In reality, we use virtually all parts of our brain every day. The brain functions as a whole system, and even simple tasks engage multiple areas simultaneously.

The brain is also closely connected to the body through the spinal cord, which serves as the central communication highway between the brain and the rest of the body. Full brain development typically occurs around age 25. On average, female brains reach full maturity between ages 22 and 24, while male brains tend to develop slightly later, around ages 23 to 25.

Understanding these facts sheds light on the powerful connection between mind and body. I remember hearing the phrase "mind over matter" as a child. At the time, it didn't quite make sense to me. Looking back, I now understand why it wasn't just that I lacked life experience but that my brain was still developing. With time, perspective, and growth, I've come to appreciate just how robust and resilient the brain truly is.

Structure of the Brain

The brain is a vital organ of the human body, much like the heart, but far more complex in both structure and function. It serves as the control center for everything we do, regulating bodily functions, processing sensory input, guiding our thoughts, and shaping our emotions. Understanding the structure and function of the brain is essential for grasping how humans think, feel, and navigate the world.

The brain is divided into three major sections, each playing a distinct and crucial role: the cerebrum, the cerebellum, and the brainstem.

The Cerebrum

The cerebrum is the most significant part of the brain and is responsible for higher cognitive functions. It is split into two hemispheres, each contributing to abilities such as planning, language, sensory perception, and reasoning. These mental activities are collectively referred to as cognitive functions.

The cerebrum is further divided into four lobes, each with specific responsibilities:

- Frontal Lobe: Involved in decision-making, emotional regulation, problem-solving, behavior control, and conscious thought.

- Parietal Lobe: Processes sensory information such as touch, temperature, and pain.

- Temporal Lobe: Plays a key role in memory, emotional processing, and auditory perception.

- Occipital Lobe: Primarily responsible for visual processing and interpreting visual information.

The Cerebellum

Located beneath the cerebrum, the cerebellum coordinates muscle movements. It also plays an essential role in maintaining balance and posture, allowing the body to perform smooth and controlled physical actions.

The Brainstem

The brainstem connects the brain to the spinal cord and is critical for sustaining life. It regulates many automatic functions, including breathing, heart rate, and blood pressure. Without the brainstem, fundamental life-sustaining processes could not occur.

Together, these three regions of the brain work in harmony to ensure that the body functions appropriately physically, mentally, and emotionally. Gaining insight into how the brain is structured helps us better understand human behavior, health, and well-being.

Brain Function

The brain serves as the body's central command center, responsible for processing information, regulating bodily systems, and enabling communication throughout the body. Among its many roles, two significant categories of brain function include cognitive and automatic processes. Additional key functions include sensory processing, emotional regulation, and motor control.

The brain receives information through the senses via sensory organs. This raw input is then interpreted, forming what we call perceptions, specifically, perceptions of our environment. This entire process is known as sensory processing. Another vital function of the brain is emotional regulation, which refers to the brain's ability to process, manage, and respond to emotional experiences. This process helps shape our behavior and mood in response to internal and external stimuli. According to the Oxford Dictionary, emotion is "a natural instinctive state of mind deriving from one's circumstances, mood, or relationship with others."

Understanding Emotions

Emotions are complex phenomena involving multiple components that shape how we experience and respond to stimuli. There are two broad categories of emotions: primary and secondary. Primary emotions are universal and biologically rooted. These include basic feelings such as happiness, sadness, fear, anger, surprise, and disgust. They are often seen as instinctual and occur as a direct response to a stimulus.

On the other hand, secondary emotions are more nuanced and culturally influenced. These emotions are more complex and can include feelings like love, pride, jealousy, guilt, and shame. Secondary emotions often arise from the interplay of primary emotions and our social, cultural, and personal experiences. Emotions play a critical role in how individuals react to the world around them. They are central to how we process information, guide our thoughts, and influence our social interactions and behaviors.

Key Components of Emotion:

1. Physiological Response: Emotions trigger physiological reactions within the body, such as increased heart rate, sweating, or trembling. For example, when someone experiences fear, they may notice their palms sweating, their face flushing, or their body shaking. These physical responses are regulated through the autonomic nervous system, which helps return the body to a state of equilibrium once the emotion has passed.

2. Subjective Experience: Emotions are deeply personal and subjective. While two individuals may encounter the same event, their emotional reactions can differ significantly. This is influenced by their past experiences, personal beliefs, and individual perspectives. How one person experiences fear, for instance, might be completely different from how another person perceives it, even in similar circumstances.

3. Behavioral Expression: Emotions are often expressed through observable behaviors. A smile, for example, is

commonly interpreted as an expression of happiness. These behavioral cues are potent indicators of how a person is feeling, and they can communicate emotional states to others. However, it's important to remember that these expressions may not always accurately reflect the complexity of the emotion itself.

Emotions also significantly impact mental and physical health. How we manage emotions can affect our decision-making, relationships, and overall well-being. Developing emotional intelligence, practicing calming techniques, or using mindfulness practices can help individuals regulate their emotional responses. In cases where emotions become overwhelming, therapy or counseling can provide valuable support, assisting individuals to gain better control over their feelings and improve their quality of life.

Emotional Functions

Emotions serve several essential functions that contribute to our survival, motivation, social well-being, and decision-making processes. One primary function of emotion is survival. Emotions like fear act as internal alarms, signaling potential threats and triggering instinctive responses such as fight, flight, or freeze. These reactions can be lifesaving, helping individuals avoid harm and respond quickly in dangerous situations.

Another crucial emotional function is decision-making. While making decisions isn't always straightforward, emotions play a critical role in guiding our choices. They influence how we evaluate options, assess risks, and align decisions with personal values. Factors such as urgency, emotional state, and a sense of competence often shape the direction we take when faced with critical choices.

Social connection is also deeply tied to our emotional life. As human beings, relationships are fundamental to our existence. Emotions help us build, sustain, and deepen connections with others. They foster empathy, enhance communication, and allow us to experience shared meaning. A lack of social connection, on the other hand, can lead to isolation and emotional distress. When expressed and managed well, emotions can strengthen bonds and create a sense of belonging.

Finally, emotions are powerful sources of motivation. Oxford defines motivation as "something that arouses action or activity. "Our emotional responses often drive motivation. Passion, excitement, love, or even guilt can inspire us to act or, in their absence, keep us from acting. Emotional motivation pushes people to set goals, take risks, or overcome obstacles, depending on how they interpret and respond to what they feel. Emotions are not just reactions; they are essential drivers of human behavior, influencing every area of life, from survival and decision-making to relationships and personal growth.

Key Body Components

The human body is composed of many interconnected parts, each playing a vital role in how we experience and express emotion. In this book, we'll focus on a select few: the brain, the head, the face, the chest (particularly the heart), the stomach, the hands, and the legs. These areas are not only essential to our biological functions but also serve as physical indicators of our inner emotional states. When the mind is grappling with various emotions, their impact often reveals itself through these specific body parts. Let's explore how each of them reflects what's happening within.

Body and Emotional Distress

The body's response to emotional distress is complex and deeply interconnected, bridging the psychological and physical. Consider this: when a person experiences a strong emotion like anger, the brain receives a signal that activates the autonomic nervous system. Specifically, the sympathetic branch of the autonomic nervous system is triggered.

This system sends stress signals throughout the body, releasing hormones such as cortisol and adrenaline. These hormones prepare the body for a fight, flight, or freeze response by increasing heart rate, blood pressure, and breathing. These physiological shifts are the body's natural way of responding to a perceived threat.

These responses, known as physiological changes, are designed for short-term survival. While temporary activation can be helpful, prolonged or chronic activation of these stress responses can lead to significant emotional and physical consequences. Over time, chronic stress can contribute to emotional distress and result in serious health issues, such as heart attacks, strokes, a weakened immune system, and respiratory challenges.

But emotional distress doesn't always show up in obvious ways. It often manifests subtly in the body through muscle tension, particularly in the neck, shoulders, and jaw. These physical expressions of stress are usually overlooked but can be just as harmful over time.

Another key area impacted by emotional distress is the digestive system. Symptoms such as stomach pain, vomiting, or irritable bowel movements can arise due to the gut-brain connection, specifically through the vagus nerve, which links the stomach and brain. The gastrointestinal system is susceptible to emotional changes, and ongoing stress can disrupt its functioning, potentially leading to long-term discomfort and complications.

Fortunately, the body also has a built-in system for recovery: the parasympathetic nervous system, often referred to as the "rest and digest" system. This system counterbalances the stress response and encourages relaxation and healing. Techniques such as mindfulness, deep breathing, and meditation help activate this calming system, allowing the body to return to a balanced state.

Mindfulness exercises, in particular, are effective in lowering cortisol levels and easing physical symptoms triggered by emotional distress. However, if distress goes unaddressed, the body may struggle to access this calming response. This ongoing tension can become a cycle, making it harder for the body to recover and restore equilibrium.

The brain plays a crucial role in how we process and respond to emotional experiences. The amygdala detects threats and initiates emotional reactions, while the prefrontal cortex helps regulate those responses, supporting rational decision-making. During emotional distress, the amygdala tends to become overactive, while the prefrontal cortex may have difficulty maintaining control. This imbalance can result in impulsive behavior and emotional dysregulation, making it harder to cope effectively.

Understanding and managing emotional distress requires self-awareness and intentional self-care. Maintaining a holistic lifestyle, eating well, exercising regularly, and following a consistent sleep schedule can significantly strengthen both body and mind. These habits enhance emotional resilience and reduce the physical toll that distress can take.

When self-regulation becomes difficult, seeking support through counseling can be a decisive step. Therapists can help identify the root causes of distress and offer tools for emotional regulation. With proper support, individuals can learn to manage their emotional responses and restore balance to their mind, body, and soul. Ultimately, recognizing the deep connection between the brain and the body is essential for promoting overall wellness. By nurturing this connection, we can better manage the cycle of emotional and physical distress and move toward lasting healing and resilience.

Psychology

Psychology is the scientific study of emotions, behaviors, and thought processes. Its primary aim is to understand how individuals interact with others and their environment. Rooted in philosophy, psychology traces its origins to ancient civilizations. Greek philosophers such as Socrates, Plato, and Aristotle explored the relationship between the mind, body, and behavior.

Modern psychology began to take form in the late 19th century, with Wilhelm Wundt widely recognized as the "Father of Psychology." In 1879, he established the first experimental psychology laboratory in Leipzig, Germany, marking a significant milestone in the field's evolution.

As psychology developed, it branched into various areas of specialization to address increasingly complex questions about the human mind and behavior. These include clinical psychology, cognitive psychology, developmental psychology, and more. Each branch focuses on a specific aspect of mental life and behavior.

Psychology plays a vital role in improving human well-being. It is instrumental in understanding mental health conditions and has contributed to enhancing learning, interpersonal relationships, and productivity. One key branch is clinical psychology, where professionals use therapeutic techniques to help individuals cope with mental health challenges such as depression, anxiety, grief, and anger.

Prominent psychologists like John B. Watson and B.F. Skinner advanced behaviorism, a school of thought centered on observable behaviors. They emphasized the role of reinforcement and punishment in shaping behavior principles that have significantly influenced education and habit formation.

At its core, psychology seeks to answer fundamental questions about why people think and act the way they do. This inquiry requires examining the complex interplay between biological, psychological, and social factors. To gather insight, psychologists employ various methods such as experiments, case studies, and surveys. These tools help inform interventions designed to support individuals in overcoming challenges.

Another influential figure, Martin Seligman, pioneered the field of positive psychology. This branch focuses on fostering resilience, gratitude, and emotional well-being to help individuals lead fulfilling lives. Additionally, psychology considers how external factors like culture influence human beliefs and behaviors.

Psychology impacts everyone, whether consciously or not. It transcends age, gender, culture, and background. Developmental psychology, for instance, supports children's growth and learning. Developmental psychologists work with parents and educators to nurture children at different stages. Adolescents and young adults may seek therapy for emotional and relational concerns, while older adults often benefit from psychological support in navigating cognitive changes and the aging process.

Industrial-organizational psychology is an area of psychology that is often overlooked. Professionals in this field help businesses create healthier work environments and enhance employee satisfaction. They may design training programs that promote a sense of unity and pride among staff in what the French call esprit de corps. Psychology is a discipline grounded in rigorous scholarly research, which ensures that findings are valid and reliable. Peer-reviewed journals such as the American Psychological Association and Psychological Science publish cutting-edge studies that shape the field's evolution.

Pioneers like Albert Bandura, known for his work on social learning theory, Abraham Maslow, creator of the hierarchy of needs, and Albert Ellis, founder of Rational Emotive Behavior Therapy, have made lasting contributions to the discipline. Their work, alongside that of many others, continues to shape the way we understand human behavior. Ultimately, psychology offers invaluable insight into human complexity and plays a pivotal role in promoting well-being.

Now that we've explored the dynamic relationship between the mind and body, it's time to shift our focus to what sustains that connection in times of difficulty: well-being, grit, and resilience. Understanding the mind-body connection gives us the foundation, but it's through the development of internal strength and sustained wellness that we truly begin to thrive. In the next chapter, we'll explore how resilience is more than just bouncing back; it's about growing forward, standing tall in the face of adversity, and nurturing a life rooted in purpose, perseverance, and wholeness.

Interactive Reflection: Mind-Body Awareness Scan

Before moving on, take a moment to pause and tune in. After every chapter of this book, we'll practice a new reflective exercise to get to know ourselves better.

So, let's begin: Find a quiet space, sit or lie down comfortably, and begin a slow mental scan of your body. Starting at your toes and rising gently to the crown of your head.

With each section you pass, ask yourself: "What am I feeling here?" Is there tightness, warmth, calm, or pressure? Then ask, "Is there an emotion tied to this sensation?" Often, our bodies whisper the truths our minds ignore. This exercise isn't about fixing anything. It's only about noticing.

As you become more fluent in the language of your body, you begin to reclaim agency over your mind. This practice builds the foundation for embodied awareness that is a crucial step in building resilience from the inside out.

Chapter 2
Well-being, Grit, and Resilience

"I learned in uniform what my ancestors already knew; resilience is not taught;
it is remembered in the bones."

- Dr. C. A. Castillo

Well-being

Well-being is a multi-dimensional concept that encompasses mental, emotional, physical, and social health. It forms the foundation for living a balanced, fulfilling life. When nurtured, well-being empowers individuals to navigate life's challenges with resilience, build meaningful relationships, and achieve personal goals.

Though it may seem abstract, well-being is deeply rooted in how we respond to everyday stressors. A person's mindset and the quality of their social interactions significantly shape their overall well-being. By understanding the various dimensions of well-being, individuals can take informed steps to improve their quality of life.

Mental and Emotional Well-being

Mental and emotional well-being are central to living a healthy, purposeful life. Emotional well-being refers to the ability to recognize, express, and regulate emotions effectively. Growing emotional resilience can involve practices such as mindfulness, meditation, journaling, and seeking professional counseling. These tools can foster a healthier mindset and improve one's ability to cope with stress.

Mental well-being includes cognitive health, problem-solving abilities, and the capacity to manage stress. When individuals prioritize their mental health, they are better equipped to maintain balance during difficult times. Promoting mental well-being requires intentional effort through self-reflection, learning, and ongoing self-care.

Physical Well-being

Physical well-being plays a critical role in overall wellness. Maintaining physical health involves regular movement, proper nutrition, and sufficient rest. Activities such as stretching, running, strength training, or even simple daily walks can strengthen the heart, boost energy levels, and elevate mood.

A well-balanced diet provides essential nutrients that fuel the body and brain, while quality sleep supports mental clarity and emotional stability. Neglecting physical well-being can increase vulnerability to stress, chronic illnesses, fatigue, and emotional burnout. A consistent physical routine is not just about appearance. It's about creating the foundation for a vibrant, resilient life.

Social Well-being

Human beings are inherently social. Strong social connections are vital to emotional and psychological health. Whether it's through family, friendships, community, or professional networks, supportive relationships promote a sense of belonging, purpose, and self-worth. A solid social support system can reduce feelings of isolation, lower the risk of depression and anxiety, and promote personal growth. Building meaningful relationships and practicing kindness are simple yet powerful ways to enrich well-being.

A Holistic Perspective

True well-being integrates all aspects of self: physical, emotional, mental, and social. It involves conscious self-awareness, consistent self-care, and compassion toward oneself and others. Achieving balance requires effort, intention, and patience. But with dedication, it is possible to create a life that is not only resilient but deeply fulfilling. Ultimately, well-being is not defined by the absence of hardship but by the presence of purpose, inner peace, and the capacity to thrive amidst life's complexities.

Grit

Grit is the unrelenting perseverance and deep commitment to long-term goals, even in the face of obstacles and setbacks. It's the inner fortitude that fuels a person to keep going when things get complex or uncertain. This drive often distinguishes those who achieve their dreams from those who give up along the way. Psychologist Angela Duckworth defines grit as "a combination of passion and persistence," a formula that plays a decisive role in both personal and professional success.

One of the core traits of grit is perseverance. Individuals with grit are not defined by failure; instead, they learn from setbacks and continue moving forward. Many of the world's most successful people, including Michael Jordan, J.K. Rowling, and Thomas Edison, have demonstrated extraordinary grit.

These individuals faced repeated failures before reaching success. Thomas Edison, for instance, failed over a thousand times before inventing the light bulb. Yet he pressed on, driven by his unwavering determination. J.K. Rowling received numerous rejections before finally publishing Harry Potter, which became a global phenomenon. Michael Jordan, once cut from his high school basketball team, turned that disappointment into motivation, eventually becoming one of the greatest athletes of all time. Their stories are reminders that without perseverance, even the most talented individuals may never fulfill their potential.

Another essential aspect of grit is having a clear sense of purpose. People with grit are deeply connected to their goals. They know who they are and what they want and are willing to stay on course no matter how long or challenging the journey becomes. Athletes train for years, often sacrificing comfort and free time to reach elite levels. Entrepreneurs dedicate long hours to building successful businesses, and military professionals commit to mastering their craft through rigorous discipline. In all these cases, talent alone is not enough; it's the steadfast commitment that genuinely makes the difference.

Grit is also closely related to resilience, the ability to bounce back from adversity. Life inevitably throws challenges our way, but those with grit view obstacles as opportunities for growth rather than roadblocks. They often operate from a growth mindset, believing that improvement is possible through sustained effort and learning. This mindset helps them stay motivated in difficult times, trusting that hard work will eventually lead to progress.

Ultimately, grit is a vital quality that contributes significantly to success across various aspects of life. It blends passion, purpose, perseverance, and resilience, enabling individuals to overcome hardship and stay committed to what matters most. While intelligence and talent are valuable, they mean little without the determination to keep pushing forward. In the end, grit often marks the line between those who achieve greatness and those who fall short.

Resilience

Resilience is the ability to bounce back after being knocked down. It also refers to the capacity to adapt, overcome, and thrive in the face of life's many challenges. These challenges may stem from emotional experiences such as stress, trauma, anger, anxiety, guilt, grief, or a combination of these and other challenging emotions.

Resilience, recognized as a key pillar of mental well-being, plays a critical role in determining how successfully an individual navigates life. It enables people to rebound from setbacks and move forward, even when life feels overwhelming.

While often used interchangeably, resilience and resiliency are not the same. Resilience refers to the outcome of the ability to recover. Resiliency, on the other hand, speaks to the traits and processes that support recovery and emotional healing. Understanding this distinction helps clarify how resilience operates on both a behavioral and psychological level.

This chapter explores the science behind resilience, highlighting individuals who have exemplified it in the face of adversity. It will also examine evidence-based strategies that foster resilience and promote long-term emotional strength.

Sometimes, a person may experience significant distress after a stressful event enough to impact daily functioning, but their symptoms may not meet the criteria for specific diagnoses like acute stress disorder or adjustment disorder. In such cases, resilience becomes even more vital in helping the individual cope and regain balance.

Resilience manifests in different forms, often referred to as the science of resilience. These include:

- Psychological resilience: the mental and emotional strength to manage stress and recover from emotional turmoil.

- Physical resilience: the body's ability to withstand and recover from illness, fatigue, or physical stress.

- Social resilience: the strength found in support systems, community connections, and relationships that help individuals navigate challenging times.

Each of these plays a role in shaping how a person responds to adversity. Together, they offer a holistic framework for understanding and building resilience in daily life.

The Science of Resilience

The first type of resilience we'll explore is psychological resilience: the ability to adapt in the face of emotional stress, adversity, or trauma. It allows a person to withstand mental and emotional challenges and bounce back stronger.

Several key factors contribute to building psychological resilience. Among them are positive thinking, cognitive flexibility, and emotional regulation. These traits help individuals navigate difficult situations with greater clarity and control.

When people hear the word resilience, they often think of grit, and for good reasons. Grit, like resilience, reflects mental toughness.

31

It's the inner strength that empowers someone to push through hardship and keep going, even when things feel overwhelming.

Physical Resilience

Physical resilience is the second key pillar of overall resilience. It refers to the body's ability to withstand and recover from physical challenges, such as illness, injury, or fatigue. Strengthening physical resilience involves building healthy habits, including balanced nutrition, regular exercise, adequate sleep, and effective stress management.

These practices not only support the body's recovery and endurance but also enhance overall well-being. The connection between mind and body plays a crucial role here. Psychological stress, for example, can impact physical health just as physical illness can affect emotional functioning. Developing physical resilience, therefore, means taking care of both the body and the mind and recognizing their deep and dynamic interdependence.

Social Resilience

The third and final dimension of resilience is social resilience: the ability to draw strength and support from relationships, community, and social networks during challenging times. Social resilience plays a critical role in how individuals cope with adversity, especially when facing hardships like financial struggles, health crises, or personal loss.

People who are deeply connected to their communities, whether through family, friendships, faith-based groups, or local organizations, tend to navigate difficulties more successfully. Strong social ties not only offer emotional support but also provide practical resources and problem-solving help in times of need. For example, individuals with solid support systems often fare better during natural disasters, as they can rely on others for shelter, information, and recovery assistance. Over the years, countless examples have shown how social bonds can be a lifeline in the face of adversity. In the following section, we'll explore a few powerful stories of individuals who exemplify social resilience in action.

Examples of Resilience

Resilience is the ability to recover from adversity, adapt to change, and keep going in the face of hardship. Throughout history, many individuals have exemplified resilience through their actions, character, and achievements. Among them are Nelson Mandela, Oprah Winfrey, and Walt Disney, three people who faced enormous challenges yet rose above them with remarkable strength and perseverance.

Nelson Mandela is a powerful example of resilience. He spent 27 years in prison for standing up against apartheid in South Africa, a system of racial segregation and injustice. Despite enduring nearly three decades of incarceration, Mandela never gave up on his vision of equality and freedom. Upon his release, rather than seeking revenge, he chose forgiveness and unity, eventually becoming the first Black President of South Africa. Mandela displayed physical endurance, psychological strength, and social grace in the face of extreme adversity.

Oprah Winfrey is another individual who has shown immense resilience. Born into poverty and subjected to childhood trauma, Oprah overcame a deeply troubled past. She rose through the ranks of television broadcasting, ultimately becoming one of the most influential and successful media personalities in the world. Her ability to persevere through emotional pain, discrimination, and professional obstacles speaks volumes about her inner strength. Like Mandela, she exemplifies resilience on physical, psychological, and social levels.

Walt Disney also demonstrated extraordinary resilience. He experienced multiple business failures and was even fired early in his career for "lacking creativity." Yet, he never gave up on his dream. Despite financial setbacks and repeated rejection, Disney continued to create, imagine, and build. His vision eventually gave birth to a global entertainment empire. His journey is a testament to resilience, the capacity to bounce back, adapt, and transform failure into lasting success.

These individuals, Mandela, Winfrey, and Disney, represent just a few examples of what it means to be resilient. There are countless others, famous and unknown, who have faced life's toughest challenges and found ways to rise above them. Resilience is not about avoiding hardship; it's about facing it head-on, learning from it, and emerging stronger. No matter what the obstacle, each of us can overcome and grow.

Beyond the GOAT Debate: A Lesson in Resilience and Appreciation

The "Greatest of All Time" (GOAT) debate stretches across all sports, from boxing and football to tennis and track. Fans passionately weigh in, comparing statistics, championships, and cultural impact in an effort to crown a singular legend. While these discussions can be entertaining, they often spiral into divisive arguments that overshadow a more meaningful takeaway: the importance of recognizing and appreciating greatness in all its forms.

This perspective is compelling in the world of basketball. Rather than fixating on who reigns supreme, we can learn from the resilience, mental strength, and leadership that legendary players have brought to the game. Icons like Michael Jordan, LeBron James, Magic Johnson, Kobe Bryant, Kareem Abdul-Jabbar, and Bill Russell each possessed unique strengths. Jordan's relentless competitiveness, LeBron's adaptability, Kobe's "Mamba Mentality," Magic's infectious leadership, Kareem's consistency and discipline, and Russell's unshakable dominance all offer different expressions of greatness. What they share is not just skill but a deep-rooted resilience, a refusal to be defined by setbacks.

Their influence goes far beyond the hardwood. LeBron's activism and educational initiatives, Magic's entrepreneurial success, and Russell's courageous stance on civil rights reveal a truth often missed in GOAT debates: true greatness is measured not only by accolades but by the impact one has on others. These athletes used their platforms to confront adversity, embrace change, and empower communities, a kind of greatness that echoes far beyond buzzer-beaters and championship rings.

In that light, perhaps the point isn't to decide who was "better" but to understand how greatness evolves. Each player built upon the legacy of those who came before, shaping the game in new and enduring ways. Likewise, in life, success isn't about comparison. It's about growth. It's about learning from those who've walked the path and paving new roads for others.

When we shift the GOAT conversation from competition to appreciation, we move from a narrow, binary mindset to one that celebrates diversity, resilience, and transformation. Greatness isn't static. It's multifaceted, evolving, and deeply human.

And it's not exclusive to sports legends. True resilience exists everywhere in the quiet strength of those fighting unseen battles and in the perseverance of individuals coping with loss, rejection, or uncertainty. The same drive that propelled Jordan or Kobe through career-defining moments is mirrored in everyday people who continue to rise despite the odds. Ultimately, the lesson is this: greatness isn't about being the best. It's about becoming the best version of yourself over and over again.

Foundation of Resilience

From the moment Dominique was born, she belonged to no one and to everyone all at once. She entered the world in a small village nestled in a third-world country, where the air was thick with the scent of rain-soaked earth and the voices of children echoed through narrow, winding paths. Her mother, bound by duty to another family, loved her in the shadows. Her father, living an ocean away, acknowledged her existence but could not claim her in the open.

Dominique was the secret no one could afford to hold too tightly. For the first six years of her life, she lived with her father's sister, Aunt Zora, a woman of quiet strength and sharp wit. Aunt Zora raised her like her own, teaching her how to balance a bucket of water on her head, knead the dough for the morning's bread, and read by the dim glow of a kerosene lamp. Dominique learned early that love wasn't always about blood; it was about who stayed when no one else would. But one evening, Aunt Zora clutched her chest and collapsed onto the earthen floor. Just like that, Dominique's world crumbled. She was alone again.

At six, she was sent to live with her father's elderly aunt, whose hands trembled with age but whose spirit remained unbroken. For three years, Dominique endured. She walked miles to school on an empty stomach, knowing that education was her only ticket out of the uncertainty she was born into. She studied by candlelight, reciting lessons to herself as she pounded cassava in the evenings.

She didn't cry when the other children whispered about how she had no real home. Instead, she pressed on, holding fast to the belief that she was meant for something more. It was during these years that she began developing grit, the quiet, persistent kind that teaches you to endure, adapt, and keep moving forward. Strength, for her, wasn't a choice. It was survival. And in that necessity, she found power.

Then, one day, a letter arrived sealed with a decision already made. Her father had arranged for her to come to the United States. Dominique was nine when she boarded the plane, alone but unafraid. She landed in a world of asphalt streets and air that smelled of gasoline and fast food instead of rain and open fire.

She went to live with her father's niece and her four children, squeezed into a house that never truly felt like home. But she adapted. She studied harder than anyone, aware that she had been given a rare chance. She swallowed her loneliness and focused on her future.

Despite everything, the nights she felt invisible, the quiet longing for her mother's embrace or her father's pride, Dominique thrived. She discovered her voice and stood tall against the weight of her past. She excelled in school, defying the odds stacked against her since birth. Her circumstances did not define her; they fueled her.

Through grit, she persevered. Through self-care, she found strength. Through resilience, she transformed pain into purpose. Dominique's childhood laid the foundation for a deeper journey of self-discovery, one that would unfold in adulthood. The lessons she learned in survival grew into emotional intelligence, mental fortitude, and the ability to weather life's storms. She didn't just survive her hardships; she transmuted them into wisdom. That wisdom would guide her choices, shape her relationships, and fuel her ambition. Though born a child of two worlds, Dominique ultimately carved out one of her own.

Having explored the foundations of resilience and the role of grit and well-being in sustaining us through life's trials, we now turn toward one of the most powerful aspects of human experience: emotion. While positive feelings lift us, it is often our negative emotions that test the strength of our mental resilience. Fear, anger, sadness, and shame can feel overwhelming, but they also carry messages, lessons, and opportunities for growth. In the next chapter, we'll begin the vital work of learning how to navigate these emotions with intention, clarity, and compassion, transforming them from obstacles into stepping stones.

Interactive Reflection: The 3 R's of Resilience Journal

Resilience doesn't arrive all at once. It builds over time, often in quiet moments of choice.

In your journal, reflect on the following:

- A recent **Roadblock** you encountered

- Your **Response** to it; emotionally, physically, or mentally

- A possible **Reframing of mind.** How could you reinterpret this moment as an opportunity for growth?

Remember, every setback holds within it a lesson, and every lesson is a seed of resilience. Let this become a habit, a gentle self-check-in that strengthens your grit.

Chapter 3
Navigating Negative Emotions

"Even in battle, fear was not my enemy. It was my teacher. Every emotion carries a message from within."

- Dr. C. A. Castillo

Understanding the Impact of Emotions on the Mind and Body

Emotions are central to the human experience. They shape how we respond to challenges, connect with others, and build resilience. Whether it's anger, anxiety, grief, or joy, understanding the role of emotions can empower us to face life's ups and downs with greater clarity, self-awareness, and strength. It's essential to recognize that emotions are temporary. Their intensity and duration can vary from person to person, but none last forever. Acknowledging this gives us the perspective needed to manage emotional waves more skillfully.

Exploring Negative Emotions

This chapter explores eleven core emotions ranging from anger and guilt to shame and skepticism. And how each one influences our well-being, grit, relationships, personal growth, and mental health. Through this exploration, we'll see that even the most difficult emotions carry messages and opportunities for transformation. The emotions we'll explore include Anger, anxiety, depression, grief, guilt, fear, trauma, shame, hurt and pain, stress, and skepticism.

Anger

Anger is a powerful and complex emotion. Often, it arises in response to perceived danger, injustice, or persistent frustration. It activates the body's fight, flight, or freeze response, preparing an individual to take action against a perceived threat or wrongdoing. While uncontrolled anger can have destructive consequences, it also holds the potential to build resilience and fuel personal growth.

At its core, anger can be a protective force. It may inspire individuals to defend themselves, assert boundaries, and face life's challenges with determination. For many, especially those who have endured adversity, anger becomes a source of motivation, a refusal to remain stagnant or accept mistreatment. Rather than succumbing to despair, they channel their frustration into meaningful action and positive change.

However, when left unchecked, anger can harm both personal well-being and relationships. Outbursts driven by hostility or aggression can leave deep emotional scars, damage connections with loved ones, and lead to long-term regret. Persistent anger also places strain on the mind and body, often resulting in stress, fatigue, elevated blood pressure, and emotional instability.

The key lies in managing anger constructively. Healthy outlets such as physical exercise, open communication, and problem-solving can help maintain emotional equilibrium. Techniques like deep breathing, mindfulness, and self-compassion are powerful tools for preventing anger from becoming overwhelming or destructive.

Anger also offers a gateway to self-awareness. By examining what provokes or triggers this emotion, individuals may uncover deeper, unresolved issues such as fear, insecurity, or unmet needs. Recognizing these internal triggers provides emotional insight and promotes healing.

Notably, anger can be expressed in different ways. It may become aggressive and harmful, or it can take an assertive, empowering form. Assertive anger enables people to advocate for themselves without resorting to harm. Throughout history, collective outrage at injustice has driven social reform and systemic change.

When directed wisely, anger transforms into a catalyst for justice and progress. Those who learn to regulate and channel their rage, gain emotional intelligence, self-control, and resilience. In doing so, they deepen their understanding of themselves and other skills that are essential for navigating life's difficulties with clarity and compassion.

Anxiety

Anxiety is a natural emotional response to uncertainty, perceived danger, or potential threats. Like anger, it triggers the body's fight, flight, or freeze response, increasing alertness and preparing us to act quickly. While anxiety can be an obstacle, it can also serve as a powerful motivator.

When managed well, anxiety helps individuals anticipate challenges, make thoughtful plans, and remain vigilant in uncertain situations. However, chronic or overwhelming anxiety can become a barrier hindering risk-taking, slowing progress, and limiting growth. Building resilience is essential for managing anxiety effectively. It involves learning to distinguish between helpful anxiety, which signals readiness, and harmful anxiety, which feeds avoidance and fear.

Grit plays a crucial role in navigating anxious experiences. People with grit persevere through challenges and self-doubt, refusing to let fear dictate their path. Anxiety often stems from a fear of failure, but those with grit reframe it as a sign of a growth mindset, not a reason to retreat. They view anxiety not as a weakness but as a signal that they are stretching beyond their comfort zones.

For instance, an athlete may feel anxious before a competition. Rather than being overwhelmed by nerves, they channel that energy into sharpening their focus and boosting performance. In this way, anxiety becomes a catalyst rather than a hindrance.

Effectively managing anxiety requires developing a growth-oriented mindset. When individuals embrace the idea that mistakes and setbacks are natural parts of learning and success, they are more likely to approach anxious moments with curiosity and courage rather than fear. This mindset enhances resilience, determination, and perseverance.

Left unchecked, however, anxiety can negatively affect mental health and overall well-being. It can lead to chronic stress, fatigue, sleep disturbances, headaches, and digestive issues. Relationships may also suffer, as anxiety-driven behaviors such as excessive worry, jealousy, or emotional withdrawal can create distance and tension.

Developing healthy coping skills is essential. Practices like mindfulness, deep breathing, journaling, or talking to a trusted friend can ease anxiety at the moment. However, individuals who continue to struggle are encouraged to seek support from mental health professionals. Therapists can offer personalized strategies and tools to help prevent anxiety from becoming a dominant force in one's life. Ultimately, overcoming anxiety is not about eliminating it but learning how to navigate it. A balanced approach grounded in self-awareness, acceptance, and action empowers individuals to move forward without being held back by fear or worry.

Depression and the Power of Resilience

Depression is more than just sadness; it's a persistent, often overwhelming sense of hopelessness, emotional exhaustion, and lack of motivation that can affect every area of a person's life. Unlike temporary feelings of sadness, depression lingers and can interfere with daily functioning, relationships, and overall well-being.

When it comes to resilience, depression presents a deep and personal challenge. It forces individuals to dig beneath the surface, to search for inner strength even when they feel completely drained. Those who build resilience in the face of depression often lean on a combination of self-care, support networks, and professional help. They come to understand that although depression can be all-consuming, it isn't permanent. Through consistent effort, individuals can develop coping strategies that serve them not only in the present but also in future moments of emotional distress.

Grit's ability to persevere through difficulty is especially vital in managing depression. For someone in the depths of it, even the most minor tasks can feel monumental. Yet, by tapping into grit, individuals can find the motivation to carry out everyday responsibilities like getting out of bed, going to work, or engaging in self-care. This steady commitment to movement, no matter how slow, plays a crucial role in long-term healing.

Resilient individuals don't ignore their struggles; they acknowledge them. But they also refuse to let those struggles define who they are. Recovery from depression isn't linear; there will be setbacks, moments of doubt, and days that feel impossible. But grit allows individuals to keep moving forward, trusting that slow progress is still progress. This persistence can eventually help restore a sense of purpose, direction, and self-worth.

For example, someone coping with depression may wrestle with feelings of worthlessness, profound fatigue, and an inability to feel joy. But with perseverance, they might still complete small goals, re-engage with parts of life they once loved, or simply show up for themselves day after day. These seemingly minor victories become milestones in a larger journey toward healing.

Depression also impacts communication and connection. It can drain the desire to engage with others and diminish interest in previously enjoyable activities. Unfortunately, symptoms of depression are often misunderstood by friends and family as laziness or disinterest, which can create further isolation.

This misunderstanding makes awareness and education critical. When depression is recognized for what it is, a legitimate mental health condition, it becomes easier for individuals to seek help without shame. Therapy, medication, emotional support, and lifestyle changes are all valid and valuable tools for managing it. The first step toward healing is often acknowledging the reality of depression without judgment.

By combining self-awareness with external support and a commitment to persevere, individuals can begin to overcome the heavy weight of depression. Though the journey may be long, it often leads to deeper personal growth, renewed strength, and a more compassionate relationship with oneself.

Grief and Resilience

Grief is an intense emotional response to loss. While it is most often associated with the death of a loved one, it can also arise from other life changes, such as relocating to a new place, losing a job, or missing out on a significant opportunity. The emotions that accompany grief can feel overwhelming and unpredictable. Often, grief manifests not just as sadness but as a complex web of secondary emotions like anger, guilt, confusion, or anxiety.

From a resilience perspective, grief becomes more than just emotional pain; it becomes a process of inner reckoning and eventual renewal. Resilient individuals recognize that healing doesn't mean forgetting the person, place, or opportunity they've lost. Instead, it involves learning how to live with the loss, to carry it, and to continue moving forward in meaningful ways.

It's important to remember that grief is a profoundly personal journey. No two people experience it in the same way, and there is no set timeline for healing. Developing healthy coping strategies such as leaning on support systems, expressing emotions openly, and finding meaning in the loss can be key components in building resilience through sorrow.

Grit, often defined as perseverance in the face of adversity, can be a powerful ally during grief. It helps individuals remain grounded and keep pushing forward, even when the weight of loss feels paralyzing. Those with grit and resilience may still struggle, but they find ways to re-engage with life. It might start with small acts, getting out of bed, showing up to work, or simply reaching out for help.

Over time, these small acts build momentum. Grieving individuals begin to reclaim their strength, take responsibility, and pursue personal goals again, even while carrying their pain. They learn that grief doesn't disappear, but it can coexist with hope, purpose, and growth.

Grief profoundly affects emotional well-being and relationships. Some people may withdraw, while others may lean more heavily on their support networks. When unaddressed, grief can harden into prolonged states of anger, depression, guilt, or anxiety.

However, when processed in healthy ways through support groups, mindfulness practices, or professional mental health care, grief can become a catalyst for profound personal transformation.

Many individuals report gaining a renewed appreciation for life, a greater sense of empathy, and a more substantial capacity to support others going through similar pain. In the end, learning to live with grief or making it manageable, rather than being consumed by it, is a vital step toward emotional healing and long-term resilience.

Guilt

Guilt is the emotional discomfort that arises when we believe we've violated our personal values or moral standards. It can be excruciating, but guilt also plays a vital role in resilience, encouraging self-reflection, accountability, and personal growth.

Resilient individuals don't allow guilt to consume or paralyze them. Instead, they use it as a catalyst for transformation. They begin by acknowledging their mistakes, taking responsibility, and making necessary amends. From there, they implement changes to avoid repeating the same missteps, turning guilt into an opportunity for learning.

From the perspective of grit, guilt can act either as a stumbling block or a source of motivation. While some allow guilt to spiral into shame, doubt, or self-sabotage, individuals with grit recognize that everyone makes mistakes. What matters is how we respond. Overcoming guilt requires self-forgiveness and a clear understanding of personal responsibility, such as owning what's yours without taking on more than necessary.

Rather than ruminating on past failures, gritty individuals focus on forward motion and are committed to becoming better versions of themselves. Take, for example, a mother who once abandoned her child at birth. Over time, her guilt may inspire her to be fully present for her other children, ensuring they feel loved, seen, and secure. Her past doesn't define her, but it informs her commitment to do better.

Unresolved guilt, however, can have profound implications for well-being. It can feed into depression, anxiety, or anger and often undermines self-worth. This emotional strain may strain relationships, leading to disconnection or feelings of unworthiness.

But when guilt is addressed with honesty, vulnerability, and self-compassion.

It can strengthen bonds and foster emotional growth. Learning to accept imperfections and view guilt not as punishment but as a teacher is essential for emotional balance and mental wellness. When approached mindfully, guilt can become a tool for healing, deeper connection, and inner strength.

Fear

Fear is a natural response to danger and uncertainty. When we encounter the unknown, our survival instincts kick in, prompting us to protect ourselves. But in the context of resilience, fear becomes more than just a reaction; it becomes a teacher. It shows us how to cope with challenges while maintaining control over our actions and emotions.

Resilient individuals don't allow fear to dictate their choices. Instead, they recognize their fear, evaluate the situation, and take deliberate steps forward. Fear often signals the presence of the unknown, and learning to embrace uncertainty fosters emotional strength and adaptability.

Grit plays a key role in overcoming fear. It drives a person to act despite anxiety or hesitation. Many successful people still experience fear; they just don't let it stop them. They understand that courage isn't the absence of fear but the determination to keep going despite it.

Take, for example, someone who feels anxious about launching a new project. Despite their fear of failure, their perseverance can push them to take calculated risks and persist even after setbacks. Facing fear regularly builds confidence. Over time, individuals learn that fear, like any other emotion, is often a temporary roadblock, not a dead end.

Fear can also impact mental health, relationships, and overall well-being. While it's essential for survival, excessive fear can lead to anxiety, depression, trauma, or chronic stress. In relationships, fear of rejection may cause people to build emotional walls and avoid vulnerability.

However, fear can be managed. With practice, individuals can reframe irrational thoughts, embrace mindfulness, and seek support through therapeutic approaches like exposure therapy. These tools can help people take risks, build trust, and grow emotionally. Fear is not the enemy; it's a part of life. When approached with awareness and intention, fear can be a powerful guide toward personal growth, strength, and self-assurance.

Trauma

Trauma is a powerful force that shapes a person's resilience, well-being, and outlook on life. Often rooted in deeply distressing experiences such as childhood neglect, physical, sexual, emotional, or psychological abuse, and profound loss, trauma can leave lasting emotional and psychological imprints. While trauma often originates in early childhood and is triggered by fear, its impact doesn't have to be permanently debilitating. Initially, it can erode one's sense of safety and self-worth. Yet, when processed and addressed intentionally, trauma can also become a foundation for inner strength and transformation. Everyone faces adversity at some point in life; what defines the outcome is how we respond to it.

Those who confront their challenges head-on, rather than avoiding them, often emerge with greater emotional resilience and an improved capacity to cope with future hardships. Key components of healing include self-compassion, self-awareness, self-validation, coping mechanisms, and a reliable support system. Together, these can help individuals reclaim their well-being and convert suffering into strength.

However, trauma can also build internal walls that obstruct personal growth. In relationships, it may manifest as difficulty trusting others or forming genuine emotional bonds. Unresolved trauma can lead to emotional detachment, fear of abandonment, avoidance, or unhealthy attachment patterns. These behaviors often stem from self-protective mechanisms developed in response to past harm.

Acknowledging the presence and influence of trauma is the first step toward healing. From there, individuals can build emotional safety, practice open and honest communication, and embrace self-compassion. Whether through supportive communities, self-help practices, or professional therapy, healing becomes more attainable when we actively engage with our pain rather than run from it.

With time and effort, trauma survivors can educate themselves, reframe their experiences, and develop tools to manage the past in the present. Instead of being defined by trauma, they begin to grow through it, transforming adversity into insight, empathy, and personal evolution.

Trauma often underpins many mental health challenges, including anger, anxiety, depression, and post-traumatic stress disorder (PTSD). Left unaddressed, it can trap individuals in cycles of distress, blocking them from living purposeful, fulfilling lives. The psychological and even physical toll of unresolved trauma should not be underestimated.

Nevertheless, healing is possible. Through therapy, mindfulness, self-care, and intentional self-acceptance, individuals can regain control over their lives. Forgiveness, especially of the self, can become a liberating force in the healing journey. When met with courage and support, trauma no longer has to be a permanent scar. It can become a catalyst for deep, lasting resilience.

Trauma touches nearly every facet of a person's life. Ignoring it can undermine mental health, resilience, and personal development. Yet within the pain lies the potential for profound growth. Those who acknowledge their trauma, seek help, and commit to self-awareness can transform suffering into empowerment. Through conscious effort, strong support systems, and unwavering commitment, individuals can reshape their stories, emerging stronger, wiser, and more vibrantly alive.

Shame

Shame is a powerful emotion rooted in the belief that we are inherently flawed or unworthy. Unlike guilt, which focuses on actions, shame targets our identity, convincing us that we are the problem. Often born from early trauma, rejection, or unmet expectations, shame thrives in silence and secrecy, quietly shaping how we see ourselves and limiting our ability to connect, trust, and feel worthy.

Carrying shame feels like a hidden weight that affects every aspect of our lives. It whispers lies of inadequacy, causes self-sabotage, and fuels unhealthy coping patterns like perfectionism, people-pleasing, and addiction. But shame is learned, and what's learned can be unlearned. Healing begins when we acknowledge shame, trace its roots, and choose compassion over self-judgment. Resilience grows when we face shame with vulnerability and turn our scars into symbols of strength.

Shame undermines grit, but resilience reclaims it. It tells us to quit, to avoid failure, and to hide. Grit reminds us that our worth is not measured by perfection but by persistence. Through honest reflection, mindful practices, and support, we learn to transform shame into self-awareness. It becomes a chapter, not the end, of our story. When we face it head-on, we reclaim our wholeness and rise stronger, grounded in the truth that we are, and have always been, enough.

Hurt and Pain

Hurt is an emotional response to feeling wronged or betrayed, often striking at the core of our self-worth. It leaves us feeling vulnerable and disconnected. Pain, while often physical, can also manifest emotionally and spiritually. Both are universal and deeply human experiences. When loss or rejection hits, the emotional weight can feel unbearable, but it's within that darkness that resilience begins to take shape.

Resilience doesn't mean avoiding pain; it means learning from it. Pain often builds walls around the heart, but by facing it, we find the strength to break through. The heaviness of hurt can feel endless, making us question our worth. Yet, it is in embracing, not suppressing, these emotions that healing begins. Pain, though temporary, teaches us about our capacity to endure and grow. A resilient mind transforms pain into purpose.

It doesn't deny suffering but uses it as fuel for growth. Just as pressure forms diamonds, emotional intensity can shape character. Resilience is built through conscious effort, acknowledging pain, learning from it, and choosing to move forward. In this way, hurt and pain become powerful catalysts, shaping stronger, wiser, and more grounded versions of ourselves.

Stress

Stress is the body's natural alarm system, a response to any demand or threat, real or perceived. When triggered, the body releases hormones like adrenaline and cortisol that prepare it for a "fight, flight, or freeze" reaction. This biological response is not inherently harmful. In fact, short bursts of stress can sharpen focus, improve reaction time, and even save lives in critical situations. However, problems arise when stress becomes chronic, lingering long after the perceived danger has passed, taxing the body's systems and clouding the mind's clarity.

Stress is not just about external pressure; it is heavily influenced by how we perceive and process challenges. Two people can face the same situation, like a job interview, a deployment, or a financial setback, and experience different levels of stress depending on their mindset, past experiences, emotional regulation, and coping tools. This makes stress both universal and deeply personal. Understanding this helps shift the focus from trying to eliminate stress entirely, which is unrealistic, to learning how to navigate it with resilience.

Resilience begins with awareness. When we recognize the early signs of stress, tight muscles, racing thoughts, and irritability, we can interrupt the cycle before it spirals. Managing stress is not about avoidance; it's about building inner strength to face challenges without becoming overwhelmed. Through mindfulness, breath control, reframing thoughts, and setting healthy boundaries, we create space between stimulus and response. That space is where resilience is born. It's where the mind learns to lead the body through adversity with strength, grace, and clarity.

Skepticism

Skepticism is the practice of questioning, doubting, or critically evaluating information before accepting it as truth. It is not the same as cynicism, which assumes the worst in people or situations. Instead, skepticism functions as a mental guardrail, helping individuals think independently, assess situations objectively, and avoid being misled by false claims, manipulation, or emotional impulses.

In a world saturated with opinions, media, and misinformation, healthy skepticism serves as a vital tool for protecting the mind from confusion and undue influence. At its core, skepticism empowers resilience. When we are skeptical, we slow down and assess rather than react. We ask questions like, Is this information accurate? What's the source? Does this align with my values and experiences? This level of critical thinking gives us more control over our decisions, actions, and beliefs.

Skepticism fosters clarity and intentionality, especially during high-stress or emotionally charged situations where impulsive thinking can lead to regret or harm. It allows us to move forward not just with emotion but with evidence, reason, and balance. However, skepticism must be measured. Too much skepticism can lead to paralysis, distrusting everyone, doubting every decision, and becoming isolated in fear or indecision.

The key is to balance skepticism with open-mindedness. A resilient mind is one that questions the world but remains teachable, adaptable, and capable of growth. When used wisely, skepticism becomes a strength, a filter, not a wall, allowing us to engage with the world thoughtfully, protect our energy, and stand firm in our truth without closing the door to new perspectives.

Dominique's Emotions: Anger

Dominique carried anger like a hidden ember, smoldering beneath the surface. She was angry at the world for making her feel like an outsider and for forcing her to prove her worth in ways other children never had to. She was furious at her father for keeping her at a distance from choosing his other family while she was left to go through life alone.

She was angry at her mother for not fighting for her, for choosing comfort over connection. That anger could have consumed her, hardened into resentment. But instead, she used it as fuel. She poured it into her studies, into her quiet resolve to become something more than an afterthought.

Still, the anger didn't always serve her well. Sometimes, it erupted without warning. A careless comment from a teacher or a dismissive glance from a classmate could spark a reaction that felt too intense, even to her. She lashed out in ways she didn't understand, slamming doors, speaking in cutting tones, and pushing people away before they could leave her. Anger, she realized, was easier than vulnerability. It was simpler to be furious than to admit she was hurt.

In time, Dominique began to confront her anger rather than let it define her. She found outlets for writing, running, and even sitting in silence and letting herself feel without judgment. Slowly, she traced her anger back to its roots: pain, grief, and a deep longing to belong.

She stopped fighting the emotion and started listening to it. Over time, she transformed it from something that consumed her to something that propelled her. Her anger became a source of strength, a force she wielded to speak up, stand her ground, and advocate for herself and others who felt unseen. What once threatened to destroy her became the fire that shaped her.

Anxiety

Anxiety crept into Dominique's life like an unwelcome guest, always lingering in the background. The fear of failure haunted her. The pressure to succeed was a weight on her chest. Every time she walked into a new space, whether a classroom, a friend's house, or even her own home, she felt like she didn't belong. She was constantly worried about saying the wrong thing, doing the wrong thing, being the wrong thing.

Her anxiety was most relentless at night. Lying in bed, she would replay conversations in her mind, analyzing every word. She worried about whether she had embarrassed herself or upset someone. She worried about the future, about whether she would ever be enough for her father to truly love her, about whether she could escape the uncertainty that had shaped her childhood. This constant state of unease was exhausting. It made her body tense, her thoughts raced, and her stomach churned.

Over time, Dominique learned that anxiety thrived on control. The more she tried to control everything, the worse it became. She began practicing mindfulness, reminding herself that she could only focus on what was within her power. She found comfort in routines, in deep breaths, and in reminding herself that she was worthy regardless of external validation. She still felt anxiety, but instead of letting it paralyze her, she acknowledged it, allowed it to exist, and then moved forward anyway.

Depression

Some days, Dominique felt nothing at all. The weight of her past, the loneliness of her present, and the uncertainty of her future drained her of any motivation to get out of bed. She moved through life like a ghost, going through the motions but feeling disconnected from everything around her. She excelled in school, but success felt hollow. She had friends, but she still felt alone. She laughed, but it never reached her soul.

Depression made her question her worth. There were moments when the weight felt unbearable, but deep down, she knew there was still a spark within her. She convinced herself that if she disappeared, no one would genuinely notice. But deep down, something inside her refused to surrender.

Dominique eventually found solace in small acts of self-care writing, talking to trusted friends, and reminding herself of how far she had come. She sought help, realizing she didn't have to carry everything alone. Over time, she learned that depression wasn't a sign of weakness; it was a battle requiring strength. She kept fighting, determined to carve out a future beyond the darkness.

Grief

Grief was Dominique's oldest companion, the silent shadow that had followed her since childhood. She grieved the mother she never truly had, the father who loved her in secret, and the childhood she spent searching for a home that never existed. She grieved for Aunt Zora, the only person who ever made her feel safe, and for the years, she was shuffled between houses, always temporary, never truly belonging.

At first, Dominique didn't know how to process grief. She pushed it down, ignored it, and convinced herself she was too strong to dwell on what she'd lost. But grief demands to be felt. It surfaced in unexpected moments with a familiar scent, a particular song, an old memory rising like a wave, threatening to pull her under.

With time, Dominique learned that grief isn't something to conquer but something to carry. She honored her losses by remembering and allowing herself to feel them by sharing stories instead of silencing them. Healing came in, speaking about Aunt Zora. She began to embrace the love she had known rather than mourn only what had been taken. Grief became a part of her, but it no longer defined her.

Guilt

Guilt weighed heavily on Dominique's soul. She felt guilty for leaving her homeland and for having opportunities her childhood friends never would. She felt guilty for not being able to love her father the way he wanted and for resenting a mother who had made impossible choices. Guilt made her question whether she deserved happiness and whether she was selfish for wanting more.

For a long time, she carried guilt like a sentence punishment for surviving, for hoping. She believed she had to suffer to make amends for the past. Eventually, however, Dominique began to see guilt differently. She wasn't abandoning her past; she was honoring it by building something better.

Rather than letting guilt consume her, she used it as a reminder to stay connected. She sent letters, visited when she could, and made sure her success was not hers alone but a tribute to everyone who shaped her journey. Guilt could be a burden, or it could be a lesson, and she chose the latter.

Fear

Fear lived inside Dominique like a whisper, constantly reminding her of the ways she could fail and the people who could leave. She was afraid of abandonment, of being forgotten, of never being enough. Fear kept her up at night, insisting that no matter how hard she worked, she would never truly belong.

It would have been easy to let fear run her life, to stay quiet, to play it safe, to settle for less. But Dominique chose differently. She made a silent decision: she would act even when afraid. She would walk into unfamiliar rooms despite the tremble in her hands. She would speak, even if her voice shook. She would take risks, even when the outcome was uncertain.

With every fear she faced, Dominique grew stronger. Fear still existed, but it no longer ruled her. It became a signal of growth, a challenge to meet. She learned that courage isn't the absence of fear; it's moving forward in its presence.

Stress

Stress had been Dominique's constant companion since childhood, woven into the fabric of her life like an unspoken burden she learned to carry. In school, the pressure to succeed felt like an invisible weight pressing down on her shoulders. She juggled multiple responsibilities, rigorous coursework, part-time jobs, and the complexities of a home that never truly felt like hers.

There were nights when exhaustion overtook her when she stared at the pages of her textbooks but could not absorb a single word. But instead of succumbing to overwhelming anxiety, Dominique developed strategies to cope. She practiced deep breathing before exams, repeated affirmations of self-worth, and reminded herself that stress was not her enemy; it was a sign that she cared.

Over time, she learned that managing stress requires balance. She carved out moments of solitude in the chaos, taking long walks after school where she could clear her mind and reflect. She began practicing mindfulness, learning to be present rather than consumed by the constant fear of failure.

When stress threatened to consume her, Dominique found solace in small rituals. She wrote in her journal, listened to music that reminded her of home, or sipped tea in the quiet of the night. These acts of self-care were not luxuries but necessities, reminders that she was more than her struggles. Stress no longer controlled her; she controlled how she responded to it.

Skepticism

Skepticism was another challenge Dominique faced, both from others and from within herself. People doubted her potential. They questioned whether a girl with her background could rise above her circumstances. Teachers hesitated before recommending her for advanced courses, employers scrutinized her heavily before offering opportunities, and even some family members whispered that she should aim lower and accept the limits of her life. At first, these doubts stung, planting tiny seeds of uncertainty in her mind. But Dominique had faced doubts her entire life, and she refused to let it define her.

She responded to skepticism with action. When someone told her she couldn't, she worked twice as hard to prove that she could. She let her achievements speak for themselves not out of a need for validation but as a personal testament to her strength. Skepticism did not discourage her; it fueled her. She developed a quiet sense of confidence, an unshakable belief in her ability, even when no one else saw it.

But the hardest skepticism to overcome was her own. There were moments when imposter syndrome crept in when she wondered if she truly deserved the opportunities she had earned. In those moments, she reminded herself of her journey, the miles she had walked as a child, the nights she had studied under candlelight, and the sacrifices she had made. She had not come this far by accident; she had fought for every step. And so, she chose to believe in herself.

Shame

Shame lived inside Dominique like a shadow, quietly convincing her that perfection was the price of love. Raised in a home where emotions were silenced and mistakes condemned, she learned to equate worth with flawlessness. So, when she failed a college exam, it didn't just sting. It shattered her. The voice in her head whispered, "You're not enough," and she believed it.

It would have been easy to let shame define her, to retreat, to wear the mask, to carry the burden alone. And for a while, she did. But Dominique chose differently. She entered therapy. She named her pain. She traced it back to childhood wounds and began rewriting the narrative. Her emotions weren't flaws; they were truths. Shame wasn't her identity; it was a wound asking for healing.

With each layer she peeled back, Dominique grew stronger. Shame still echoed at times, but it no longer had power over her. She returned to school, reconnected with purpose, and turned her healing into a path for others. She learned that resilience isn't born from shame's silence; it's built by daring to speak, feel, and rise anyway.

Hurt and Pain

Pain lived inside Dominique like a quiet ache, etched into her bones from the moment she understood she was unclaimed. Love, for her, came in fragments, hidden, distant, and always conditional. She was a child born of secrecy, passed between homes like a borrowed thing, never quite belonging. The loss of Aunt Zora only deepened the wound, teaching her grief before she fully knew joy.

It would have been easy to let pain harden her, to shut down, to numb, to believe she was undeserving. And for a time, she did. But Dominique chose differently. She turned to books, to discipline, to grit. She built a life with her own hands, even when her heart still ached with the weight of being unwanted.

The pain didn't disappear, but it no longer defined her. She faced it, held it, and honored it. She stopped running from the shadows and stood still long enough to understand them. In doing so, Dominique found strength not in forgetting her pain but in accepting it. Her hurt became her fuel. Her scars became her story. Slowly, she became the woman her younger self needed: resilient, grounded, and whole.

Trauma

Trauma is a wound that lingers, shaping how we see ourselves, others, and the world. For Dominique, trauma wasn't one event. It was a lifetime of experiences that chipped away at her sense of safety and self-worth. It was the quiet nights spent wondering why she wasn't enough for her parents to stay. It was the instability, the survival mode she lived in, just to make it through each day.

Trauma made her hyper-aware of tone shifts, silences, and moments when love felt like it could disappear. It made her question whether she was genuinely lovable or if pain was the only thing she'd ever understand.

For years, Dominique did what so many survivors do. She buried the pain. She told herself she was fine. She believed that moving on meant never looking back. But trauma doesn't vanish. It lodges in the body, in the mind, in the soul. It showed up as anxiety in her mistrust of others, in the way she avoided vulnerability out of fear. It showed up in relationships, where she either pushed people away or clung too tightly, desperate to prove she was worth staying for.

Trauma shaped her resilience, but it also built walls around her heart. Healing meant facing what she had spent years running from. It wasn't linear. It wasn't fast. But it was possible. Therapy, mindfulness, and reflection helped her name the pain she once ignored. She began to see her past not as proof of brokenness but as evidence of survival. Slowly, she learned to soften, to trust, and to feel without drowning. Trauma had shaped her, but it did not define her. She was more than her wounds. She was her healing, her growth, and her decision to rise.

While understanding and managing negative emotions is essential for resilience, it is equally important to recognize the transformative power of positive emotions. Where sadness and fear reveal our wounds, emotions like joy, gratitude, love, and hope offer pathways to healing and renewal. They not only elevate our mood but expand our capacity to think clearly, connect deeply, and live meaningfully. As we move into the next chapter, we'll explore how cultivating positive emotions can build inner strength, enhance our overall well-being, and serve as vital fuel for navigating life with purpose and intention.

Interactive Reflection: Name It to Tame It

Emotions are not enemies. They are messengers, asking for your attention, not your resistance.

Think of an emotion that's visited you recently. It may perhaps be anger, grief, or fear. Now gently ask:

- What triggered this emotion?

- How did it feel in my body?

- What did I do in response?

When we name emotions, we disarm their power. We stop reacting and begin responding. This is emotional literacy in action and emotional resilience in motion.

Chapter 4
The Power of Positive Emotions

"Joy, love, and hope are not weak; they are the spiritual armor of the resilient mind."

- Dr. C. A. Castillo

Happiness is a positive emotional state characterized by joy, contentment, and a sense of fulfillment. While many people pursue happiness as a life goal, it's essential to recognize that happiness is often fleeting and influenced by both internal and external factors. Even so, happiness can provide emotional energy that helps individuals navigate life's challenges. Those who practice gratitude and find joy in the small things tend to be more resilient. They focus on what's going well rather than dwelling on adversity, which strengthens their ability to maintain a positive outlook.

Resilient individuals often "hunt the good stuff," seeking the silver lining in difficult circumstances. But resilience doesn't mean avoiding discomfort; instead, it's about maintaining hope and optimism in the face of hardship. An essential ingredient in long-term happiness is grit. Contrary to the belief that happiness comes from avoiding struggle, true fulfillment is often the result of enduring challenges and finding purpose within them. For example, an athlete who trains diligently for years may feel profound happiness after a hard-earned victory far deeper than someone who wins without effort. In this way, happiness is closely tied to effort, purpose, and meaning.

This connection between hard work and happiness is a recurring theme among individuals who prioritize long-term fulfillment over instant gratification. Happiness is also associated with better physical health, reduced stress, and stronger relationships, all of which contribute to a sense of well-being.

However, the pursuit of happiness can become misguided if it's rooted in materialism or external validation. Sustainable happiness stems from purpose, meaningful relationships, self-acceptance, and self-compassion. Ultimately, happiness is not a destination but a journey, one that involves developing emotional balance and the ability to adapt to life's ups and downs.

Joy

Joy is often mistaken for happiness, but it's a more profound and more enduring emotion. While external events usually shape happiness, joy originates from within and is rooted in gratitude, purpose, and love. People who experience joy tend to focus on meaningful connections and personal growth rather than constant pleasure. For instance, someone may feel joy through acts of service or by supporting a loved one, even during tough times. This joy stems from a sense of purpose and inner peace.

Joy is not about feeling good in the moment; it's about finding fulfillment through life's more profound experiences. People who cultivate joy often develop resilience by transforming challenges into opportunities for growth. Consider a musician who has struggled for years to master his craft. When he finally plays a complex piece flawlessly, the sense of joy he feels is profoundly earned through persistence, emotional strength, and dedication. This kind of joy is enduring and rooted in meaning.

Joy has a powerful impact on mental health. It improves emotional regulation, strengthens the immune system, and reduces stress. Unlike fleeting emotions like pleasure or satisfaction, joy is sustained over time and closely linked to love, spirituality, and personal values.

By practicing mindfulness, nurturing meaningful relationships, and embracing gratitude, people can cultivate joy even during challenging moments. Finding beauty in simple experiences like a heartfelt conversation or a peaceful walk can shift one's mindset and nourish emotional well-being.

Love

Love is one of the most powerful and complex human emotions. It's characterized by affection, care, connection, and deep emotional bonds. Love manifests in many forms, such as romantic relationships, family, friendship, and even self-love. Love provides a vital source of strength during hardship. When people feel supported and loved, they're more likely to persevere through difficult times. For instance, someone facing a health crisis may draw strength from the love of a family member, which can provide hope and motivation to keep going.

Love fosters emotional stability and creates a sense of belonging. This stability can serve as a foundation for growth, making it easier to navigate life's challenges. Love also inspires determination. A parent who loves their child may make enormous sacrifices to secure a better future for them, driven by deep emotional investment and commitment.

Emotional investments like this build resilience. Loving relationships offer a safe space for vulnerability and healing. When people know they're not alone in their struggles, they're better equipped to face life's setbacks.

Love is essential to well-being and mental health. Those who feel loved and valued are more likely to experience joy, reduced anxiety, and greater life satisfaction. Love fosters emotional security, reduces loneliness, and enhances communication, empathy, and conflict resolution in relationships.

Moreover, love promotes self-care. Individuals who practice self-love are more inclined to prioritize their physical and emotional needs, which contributes to long-term well-being. Whether directed inward or outward, love empowers individuals to grow, connect, and thrive.

Compassion

Compassion is a deep feeling of empathy and care for those who are suffering. It often includes not just understanding their pain but also asking: Who are they? How can they love themselves? How can they learn to be kind and forgive themselves? Compassion isn't just a passive feeling; it comes with a desire to help and alleviate the suffering of others.

Compassion involves an emotional connection to another's struggle paired with a willingness to act. It can also help individuals cope with their own difficulties by connecting with others and offering support. Those who practice compassion not only build stronger relationships but also develop greater emotional resilience.

It is about helping others build a sense of purpose, meaning, and emotional strength. For example, a caregiver tending to an ill loved one may face emotional and physical exhaustion. Yet, their compassion becomes the strength that carries them through, strengthening their grit.

Compassion influences grit by nurturing a sense of responsibility that extends beyond oneself. People with grit often channel their determination into caring for others. Compassion motivates individuals to persevere, knowing their actions can positively impact another's life. Take a teacher with a compassionate heart. They may go above and beyond to support struggling students. This is resilience in action: showing up, despite obstacles, with care and encouragement.

Compassionate people are more likely to endure hardship because their focus shifts from self to others. This outward focus stabilizes their emotions and fuels their determination. Practicing compassion significantly improves mental health and well-being. It promotes meaningful relationships and creates a sense of belonging. Interestingly, the more individuals show compassion toward others, the more they learn to treat themselves with kindness, understanding, and forgiveness.

Compassion is linked to reduced stress, better emotional regulation, and even improved physical health. Those who practice it regularly tend to experience greater life satisfaction and emotional strength. In the end, compassion becomes not just a gift to others but a powerful force for personal growth and fulfillment.

Gratitude

Gratitude is the emotion of appreciation and thankfulness for life's blessings, both big and small. It means recognizing what's good and acknowledging where that goodness comes from, whether from people, nature, faith, or circumstance. Gratitude empowers people by shifting their focus to what's working in their lives instead of what's missing. During difficult times, it can be a powerful emotional anchor. Someone grieving a loss may still find gratitude in the support of family and friends. This awareness helps keep them grounded.

Gratitude inspires motivation, endurance, and perspective. People with grit draw strength from gratitude to stay focused on their goals. It reminds them why they started and what really matters. For instance, an entrepreneur grinding away on a startup might remain driven by their gratitude for the opportunity to pursue a dream.

Gratitude brings emotional clarity. It sharpens focus on values, reinforces persistence, and can turn small blessings like waking up in the morning or providing for a loved one into sources of daily strength. The benefits are profound. Gratitude boosts mood and increases resilience, improves physical health, and promotes better emotional well-being. It promotes a positive outlook and reduces stress, anxiety, and depression.

Gratitude also strengthens relationships by nurturing appreciation and kindness. It fosters deeper connections and more supportive social bonds. Regularly practicing gratitude leads to more emotional balance and life satisfaction, making it one of the most powerful habits for living a meaningful life.

Hope

Hope is a powerful emotional state rooted in the belief that things can get better even when they're hard. It keeps people going when life gets tough and uncertainty clouds the path forward. Hope matters because it fuels the mental strength needed to pursue goals, especially when the outcome isn't guaranteed.

Resilient people rely on hope like emotional fuel. It helps them act, stay optimistic, and believe in better days. For example, someone stuck in a demanding job might keep moving forward, holding on to the hope that persistence will lead to change and growth.

Hope and grit are tightly connected. Grit needs hope to survive. Hope sustains individuals through setbacks, reminding them that the struggle is part of a longer journey. It keeps the big picture in view and reinforces belief in eventual success.

Take someone who's failed multiple times while trying to start a business. Hope keeps people going. It says, "Keep showing up. This will pay off." Without that belief, grit would lose its power because there would be no reason to keep trying.

Hope positively affects relationships, emotional health, and physical well-being. People who live with hope report greater joy, gratitude, and resilience. They bounce back from challenges faster and remain open to growth. In relationships, hope becomes a shared foundation that allows couples, families, or communities to endure and evolve together. Ultimately, hope provides emotional flexibility and the belief that change is possible. It gives people the courage to believe in their future and the strength to face adversity with faith.

Relief

Relief is the emotional release that comes when a burden lifts. It often follows a period of stress, tension, or anxiety and brings with it a wave of calm and clarity. Relief is vital. It helps people bounce back after challenges and reset their emotional state.

Take the example of a student anxious about a big exam. Once the test is over, the stress fades, and relief sets in. That emotional reset creates space for rest, reflection, and recharging before the next hurdle.

Relief reminds us that tough times are temporary. It reinforces the idea that we are stronger than our struggles. And for people with grit, relief marks the reward after enduring a storm.

It's not the absence of challenge that builds resilience. It's the process of pushing through, followed by the emotional release that comes afterward. A marathon runner doesn't just feel relief at the finish line; they feel validated. That deep sigh isn't just physical; it's spiritual. It says, "I made it."

Relief plays a key role in emotional and physical recovery. It helps people find balance again after stress, trauma, grief, or hardship. Experiencing relief lowers cortisol levels, improves immune function, and provides the mental clarity needed to move forward.

Relief is often overlooked, but it's a powerful part of the cycle of endurance. Without it, burnout takes root. With it, people heal, regain perspective, and return to life with renewed strength.

Content

Contentment is a state of inner peace that arises from appreciating the present moment while still striving for personal growth. It is not complacency but a mindful balance between ambition and gratitude. Resilience and grit play a crucial role in sustaining contentment. They empower individuals to pass through setbacks without losing their sense of fulfillment. By developing the capacity to withstand life's challenges and continue moving forward, people deepen their appreciation for the journey itself.

True well-being stems from the understanding that struggle is an inherent part of life. Content enables individuals to embrace both success and hardship with acceptance and purpose. It allows one to meet life as it is, not merely as they wish it to be.

Strong relationships are foundational to contentment. Human connection offers support, love, and encouragement. Fulfillment in relationships is nurtured through mutual respect, effective communication, and a shared willingness to grow. When individuals prioritize appreciation over comparison or resentment, their connections flourish.

Improving emotional intelligence and promoting meaningful interactions strengthens satisfaction in both personal and professional settings. A solid support system enhances mental wellness and reinforces the truth that fulfillment is not solely found in material success but in shared emotional experiences. Content nurtures personal growth and mental health when embraced as a guiding principle. A growth mindset, paired with self-acceptance, encourages people to pursue their goals without constant self-criticism. It allows them to celebrate progress rather than fixate on perceived shortcomings, promoting a healthier self-image and reducing anxiety.

Practicing mindfulness, gratitude, and self-care helps build the foundation for lasting happiness. When resilience, meaningful relationships, and commitment to well-being are integrated into everyday life, contentment transforms from a distant concept into a sustainable way of being. By engaging with narratives that normalize struggle and celebrate progress, individuals develop a balanced, empowered perspective.

Eustress

Eustress, or positive stress, is a powerful catalyst for resilience, grit, and well-being. Unlike distress, which can overwhelm and paralyze, eustress propels individuals beyond their comfort zones, inspiring personal growth. It enhances resilience by teaching individuals to manage pressure without breaking. This reframing allows people to view challenges not as threats but as opportunities for development. Eustress fortifies the perseverance required to achieve long-term goals, which promotes determination in the face of difficulty.

When correctly managed, eustress benefits mental health by providing a sense of purpose, motivation, and accomplishment. In relationships, eustress can strengthen bonds and encourage healthy communication. Navigating challenges together, resolving conflicts, setting mutual goals, or facing life's hurdles builds deeper trust and understanding. Couples, friends, and colleagues who approach stress as a shared experience often emerge stronger and more connected.

Eustress also promotes growth in social settings. Stepping outside of comfort zones leads to new experiences and meaningful connections. When viewed as a tool for connection rather than a force of division, stress becomes a constructive element in relationships.

Eustress thrives on personal growth and mental wellness. It encourages individuals to pursue new skills, physical goals, or career aspirations. Rather than stagnating, they remain engaged and motivated. By learning to channel stress constructively, people develop a stronger sense of confidence and adaptability. Embracing eustress as a positive force helps individuals build a life of purpose, progress, and fulfillment.

Dominique's Journey Continues

Happiness was a complex emotion for Dominique. Sometimes, it felt fleeting, like a flash of sunlight before another storm. But through resilience, she learned that happiness wasn't about a flawless life. It was about discovering joy in imperfection. She began to celebrate small victories: passing an exam, making a friend, feeling the sun on her skin. She realized happiness wasn't something that happened to her. It was something she created.

Her grit enabled her to fight for joy, even when life tried to steal it. She didn't wait for perfect conditions. She found joy in everyday moments. She laughed through the pain, danced when no one was watching, and found comfort in simply being alive. Happiness became her rebellion, a refusal to surrender.

Gratitude became her compass. Dominique practiced reflection, acknowledging her achievements and the people who stood by her. She discovered happiness wasn't a destination but a mindset. One grounded in resilience, self-love, and the courage to embrace life fully.

For Dominique, joy ran deeper than happiness. While happiness was sometimes dependent on external conditions, joy stemmed from within. She found it in quiet, meaningful acts: helping a classmate, receiving kindness from a teacher, and watching the sunrise. Joy became her strength, her anchor in darkness.

Her grit helped her seek purpose in pain. She didn't allow hardship to blind her to beauty. She found joy in growth, in the realization that she was evolving into the person she was meant to be.

To sustain this joy, Dominique embraced practices that nurtured her spirit, spending time in nature, creating art, and developing meaningful relationships. She realized joy wasn't the absence of pain;

it was resilience's companion, whispering, "There is still something worth holding on to."

Love was perhaps Dominique's most complicated lesson. She had seen it in many forms, some beautiful, others painful. Ultimately, she discovered real love begins within. She learned to love herself despite her past and accept her worth without conditions. Love wasn't just about others. It was about the relationship she built with herself.

With grit, she broke free from toxic patterns. She no longer craved validation from others. Instead, she validated herself. She established boundaries and chose relationships that nurtured rather than drained her. Love became an act of self-respect.

For her well-being, love became a source of healing. It wasn't about perfection; it was about forgiveness and acceptance. She opened her heart again, even after pain. Love surrounded her in friendships, mentorships, and even the kindness of strangers. Most of all, it lived in her growing belief that she was worthy of love just as she was.

Compassion was another gift Dominique embraced, not just for others but also for herself. After years of guarding her emotions, she once saw vulnerability as a weakness. But she eventually realized that her true strength was in empathy and connection.

Her grit allowed her to practice compassion even when it was difficult. She forgave not because others deserved it but because she refused to let their actions define her. She chose to uplift others, mentoring younger students who, like her, had faced adversity. Her pain became a bridge, not a wall.

Dominique practiced self-compassion. She learned to rest when needed and speak to herself with kindness. Healing, she understood, wasn't just about pushing through. It was about honoring her emotions. Through compassion, she deepened her capacity to love and be loved.

Gratitude became Dominique's anchor in life's storms. For years, she focused on what was missing: family, stability, and belonging. But she eventually shifted her lens. Instead of dwelling on lack, she counted her blessings: a sharp mind, a resilient body, and friends who became family.

Her grit helped her make gratitude a habit. Even on hard days, she identified small wins. She kept a gratitude journal, noting three things each night. Over time, this reshaped her outlook. She learned to see life through a lens of abundance.

Gratitude brought her peace. It didn't erase hardship but made it bearable. It reminded her that even in darkness, there was light worth seeking.

Hope was Dominique's north star. Life had taught her that hardship was inevitable, but so was possibility. Hope was not just an emotion; it was a choice—a decision to believe in a brighter future.

Her resilience grew from this belief. In moments of rejection or loneliness, she reminded herself that setbacks were temporary. She dreamed boldly and pursued her goals with fierce determination. Hope gave her fuel.

For her well-being, hope offered purpose. It made mornings meaningful. She surrounded herself with hopeful people and mirrored their optimism. She learned that hope isn't passive; it's something you build moment by moment.

Dominique rarely gave herself permission to feel relief. Survival often left little room to breathe. But when she achieved something, getting into college, earning a scholarship, or simply making it through the day, relief washed over her.

Her resilience allowed her to embrace these moments. She began recognizing her victories, however small. Relief wasn't weakness; it was a sign of strength. A milestone was reached. For her well-being, relief became an act of self-care. She celebrated wins, honored her progress, and allowed herself to rest. In doing so, she found balance.

Contentment was once a foreign concept to Dominique, who had spent years striving. But over time, she realized that contentment was not about settling; it was about peace. She found it in quiet moments, in the knowledge that she had done her best. It lived in friendships, laughter, and the warmth of a safe space.

Her grit taught her that contentment wasn't the enemy of ambition. It was its companion. She learned to hold gratitude and drive in harmony. She found joy in the present while working toward the future. She practiced mindfulness, living in the now, embracing self-acceptance, and trusting that contentment comes from within.

Eustress, the positive force of pressure, became a catalyst for Dominique. It pushed her to grow. Whether preparing for exams, training for a marathon, or chasing a dream, she thrived under pressure.

Her resilience helped her distinguish stress from burnout. She saw challenges as proof of her strength. For her well-being, she created routines that supported balance. Exercise, meditation, and strategic goals became part of her life. She remembered what her Aunt Zora said: "Pressure breaks pipes, but it also creates diamonds."

This chapter explored positive emotions and how Dominique integrated them into her life despite adversity. The next chapter will focus on practical tools individuals can use to cope with various emotions.

Interactive Reflection: Gratitude in Detail

Gratitude isn't just a feeling; it's a strategy. A tool for re-centering the mind when chaos looms.

- List 3 specific things you're thankful for today, small or large, ordinary or extraordinary. Next to each one, write a few lines about how it shifted your energy or changed your perception.

- Don't rush. Savor the memory. Let your nervous system soak in the safety and joy that these moments created. In doing so, you reinforce positive neural pathways, turning gratitude into resilience.

Chapter 5
Tools for Coping with Emotions

"Healing begins with small choices, stillness, nourishment, movement, and community. That's how warriors rest."

- Dr. C. A. Castillo

Every day, people experience a wide range of emotions, from joy and excitement to anger, sadness, and anxiety. In the previous chapters, we explored some of these emotional experiences. In this chapter, we'll discuss practical tools that can help manage and regulate these emotions in healthy, constructive ways.

These tools are not a substitute for professional mental health care. However, they can serve as helpful strategies to promote emotional resilience, calm the mind, and support overall well-being. When practiced consistently, these techniques can empower individuals to regain control over their thoughts, improve emotional regulation, and lead more intentional lives.

Mindfulness and Meditation

One of the most powerful tools for emotional well-being is mindfulness and meditation. These practices enhance self-awareness, reduce stress, and promote a deeper sense of peace and presence in daily life. Mindfulness is the act of being fully present and engaged in the current moment, aware of your thoughts, emotions, bodily sensations, and surroundings without judgment. It means observing what is happening internally and externally without clinging to or avoiding the experience.

Mindfulness requires a conscious choice. A person can choose to remain in a state of anxiety, depression, or distress or intentionally shift focus to the present moment. Mindfulness and intense emotional states like anxiety cannot coexist fully in the same mental space. For instance, when someone feels anxious, they can choose to engage in a mindful activity to shift their focus and calm the nervous system.

Meditation, a structured form of mindfulness, involves sitting or lying in a quiet space and gently focusing the mind, often on the breath, a word or phrase (mantra), or bodily sensations. When distractions arise, attention is gently redirected. While meditation is a formal practice, mindfulness can be infused into daily activities like eating, walking, listening to music, or engaging in conversation.

Steps for Practicing Mindfulness Meditation:

1. Find a quiet space to minimize distractions.

2. Adopt a comfortable posture, either sitting upright or lying down.

3. Focus on the breath, taking slow, deep inhales and exhales.

4. Observe thoughts without judgment, allowing them to pass like clouds in the sky.

5. Consider guided imagery or using mindfulness apps for support.

6. Incorporate mindfulness into daily life, such as mindful eating, walking, or dishwashing, focusing entirely on the experience.

Types of Meditation:

- Focused Attention Meditation: Concentrating on a single object that is important to you, such as the breath.

- Loving-Kindness Meditation: Growing compassion for yourself and others.

- Body Scan Meditation: Gradually bring attention to different parts of the body to release tension.

When to Practice Mindfulness:

- Morning routine: Set a calm tone for the day.

- Stressful situations: Pause and respond mindfully.

- Before essential events: Gain clarity and focus.

- At bedtime: Calm the mind for restful sleep.

- Throughout daily activities: Stay present and connected.

When integrated consistently, mindfulness and meditation can support emotional stability, clarity, and inner peace. These practices are accessible, simple, and profoundly transformative over time.

Journaling and Self-Reflection

Journaling is a powerful tool for emotional processing, self-expression, and personal growth. It involves writing down thoughts, feelings, experiences, and reflections, creating a safe space to explore inner experiences, and tracking mental well-being over time.

Whether done through free writing, structured prompts, gratitude lists, or bullet journaling, this practice helps individuals gain clarity, reduce emotional overwhelm, and develop greater self-awareness.

Steps for Developing a Journaling Habit:

1. Choose a medium: A notebook, app, or digital document.

2. Set a routine: Daily, weekly, or as needed.

3. Use prompts or free-write: Respond to questions (e.g., "What am I thankful for today?") or simply let thoughts flow.

4. Experiment with styles: Try gratitude journaling, stream-of-consciousness writing, or reflective entries.

5. Review and reflect: Revisit past entries to notice patterns and personal growth.

Popular Journaling Approaches:

- Gratitude Journaling: Listing what you're thankful for to foster a positive mindset.

- Bullet Journaling: Organizing tasks, goals, and thoughts in a creative, structured format.

- Reflective Journaling: Processing events, emotions, or decisions with insight.

When to Journal:

- Morning reflection: Set intentions and clarity for the day.

- After stressful events: Process emotions and restore balance.

- Before bedtime: Release mental clutter for better sleep.

- During life transitions: Navigate change with grounded self-awareness.

- When overwhelmed: Regain focus by expressing and organizing thoughts.

Journaling offers a practical and personal method for exploring emotions and fostering emotional resilience. Whether used as a creative outlet or mental health tool, it creates space for honest reflection and growth.

Exercise and Physical Activity

Exercise is not only good for physical health; it's a powerful coping strategy for emotional well-being. From walking and dancing to yoga and strength training, physical activity helps regulate mood, boost energy, and build mental resilience.

When you exercise, your brain releases endorphins, which are natural mood lifters. Exercise also improves sleep, increases focus, reduces symptoms of anxiety and depression, and builds a sense of accomplishment.

Ways to Use Exercise for Emotional Wellness:

1. Identify goals: Stress relief? Energy boost? Mental clarity?

2. Choose enjoyable activities: Dancing, swimming, walking, cycling, etc.

3. Establish a routine: Aim for 30 minutes several times a week.

4. Start small: Begin with light activities and build up gradually.

5. Try mind-body movement: Yoga, tai chi, and Pilates connect physical activity with mental calm.

6. Use exercise as immediate relief: Quick walks or jumping jacks can reset the mind.

7. Make it social: Exercise with friends or support groups.

8. Stay hydrated and listen to your body to prevent burnout or injury.

9. Use technology: Fitness apps and trackers can provide structure and motivation.

When to Exercise:

- Morning: Boost energy and set a positive tone.

- During stress: Redirect nervous energy and calm the body.

- After emotional events: Reset mentally and physically.

- Before bed: Light stretching can promote relaxation.

- When overwhelmed: Get out of your head and into your body.

- During life changes: Establish structure and control in uncertain times.

No matter the time or intensity, regular physical activity supports both body and mind, making it a foundational tool for emotional coping and resilience.

Healthy Nutrition for Mental Clarity

What we eat profoundly affects how we feel. Healthy nutrition provides the body and brain with essential nutrients needed to regulate mood, support focus, and reduce emotional instability.

A balanced diet includes whole foods, fruits, vegetables, whole grains, lean proteins, and healthy fats while minimizing processed foods, sugars, and artificial additives. Nutrient-dense eating fuels both physical health and mental clarity.

Ways to Practice Healthy Nutrition:

1. Eat a balanced diet: Incorporate carbs for energy, protein for repair, and fats for brain function.

2. Prioritize whole foods: Fresh, minimally processed ingredients support long-term health.

3. Stay hydrated: Drink water consistently throughout the day.

4. Plan meals: Meal prep helps prevent poor dietary choices.

5. Eat mindfully: Slow down, savor food, and listen to hunger cues.

6. Watch portion sizes: Use smaller plates and pause between servings.

7. Reduce processed foods and sugar: Avoid mood crashes and energy dips.

8. Incorporate Omega-3s: Found in fish, seeds, and nuts, support brain and emotional health.

9. Support gut health: Use probiotics and fiber to improve digestion and mental balance.

10. Eat for stress resilience: Foods rich in magnesium, B vitamins, and antioxidants help reduce anxiety and support focus.

When combined, these four tools, mindfulness, journaling, exercise, and healthy eating, offer a strong foundation for coping with emotions and building emotional resilience. Each practice can be adapted to fit different lifestyles, preferences, and moments of need.

By using these strategies intentionally and consistently, individuals can create a toolkit for mental wellness that not only helps regulate emotional struggles but also promotes long-term health, clarity, and peace of mind.

The Importance of Adequate Sleep

Adequate sleep refers to the amount and quality of rest necessary for optimal physical and mental functioning. While sleep needs vary by age, most adults require seven to nine hours of quality sleep each night. Proper rest involves progressing through various sleep stages, including deep sleep and Rapid Eye Movement (REM) sleep, which are essential for brain function, emotional regulation, and overall well-being.

Sleep supports the body's ability to repair itself, consolidate memories, regulate hormones, and manage stress. Inadequate sleep can impair cognitive function, weaken immune response, increase irritability, and raise the risk of chronic conditions such as heart disease, obesity, and anxiety disorders.

Establishing healthy sleep habits can significantly improve mental and physical health. One of the most effective strategies is maintaining a consistent sleep schedule, going to bed, and waking up at the same time every day, which helps regulate the body's internal clock.

Creating a relaxing bedtime routine also encourages restful sleep. Engaging in calming activities like reading, journaling, or taking a warm bath signals the body that it's time to wind down. Limiting exposure to blue light from phones, computers, and tablets before bed can enhance melatonin production, improving sleep quality.

Optimizing the sleep environment is another crucial step. Keeping the bedroom dark, quiet, and calm can promote more profound, more restorative sleep. Avoiding stimulants such as caffeine, nicotine, and heavy meals before bedtime can also prevent disruptions.

Incorporating regular physical activity into your routine helps regulate sleep patterns, though it's best to avoid vigorous exercise close to bedtime. Additionally, managing stress through mindfulness, deep breathing, or reflective journaling can quiet the mind and make it easier to fall asleep.

Limiting naps, especially in the late afternoon or evening, supports better nighttime sleep. While short power naps can be refreshing, long or irregular naps may interfere with your natural sleep cycle.

Adequate sleep is essential during critical life situations. High-stress periods such as facing personal challenges, tight work deadlines, or academic exams require mental clarity and emotional stability, both of which are supported by good sleep.

Following emotional or traumatic events, sleep is vital for healing and emotional processing. Similarly, maintaining a consistent sleep routine can help regulate mood and reduce symptoms of anxiety, depression, and other emotional disturbances.

After intense physical activity, sleep aids in muscle recovery reduces inflammation, and enhances performance. It is equally crucial before making significant decisions or tackling complex problems, as a well-rested mind is better equipped for rational thinking.

Life transitions, such as moving, changing jobs, or experiencing loss, can be emotionally draining. Adequate sleep during these periods provides the stability needed to adapt. Additionally, consistent sleep strengthens immune function, improving the body's ability to fight illness and recover from infections.

Prioritizing sleep is essential for managing stress, enhancing emotional regulation, and building resilience. Proper sleep habits contribute to a more balanced, energized, and focused mind, ultimately supporting better overall health and well-being.

Building a Strong Social Support System

Social support refers to the emotional, psychological, and practical assistance received from friends, family, colleagues, and community networks. It fosters a sense of belonging, reduces stress, and enhances overall well-being by offering comfort, encouragement, and resources during difficult times.

Research shows that individuals with strong social support experience lower levels of stress, anxiety, anger, and depression. These connections are essential for emotional resilience and mental health. In contrast, the absence of support can make individuals more vulnerable to emotional distress, increasing the risk of self-injury or harmful behaviors.

Social support generally falls into four main categories: emotional, instrumental, informational, and companion support. Emotional support offers empathy, reassurance, and care. Instrumental support involves practical help, such as transportation or financial aid. Informational support provides advice and guidance, while companion support includes shared activities and the comfort of companionship.

To effectively utilize social support, it's essential to identify your support system, communicate openly, and seek help proactively. Join structured support networks such as therapy groups, online forums, or community organizations to connect with others facing similar challenges.

Offering support to others strengthens relationships and fosters mutual growth and purpose. Building reciprocal relationships creates a lasting foundation for resilience and emotional strength. Professional support from therapists, counselors, or social workers can also provide specialized help beyond what friends and family can offer.

Social support is particularly valuable during significant life transitions, stressful periods, and when facing mental health challenges. It's also beneficial for daily coping, building long-term resilience, and enhancing emotional strength.

Significant life changes like starting a new job, moving, or grieving a loss can be overwhelming. In these moments, social support eases the emotional burden and facilitates adjustment. During crises or emotional distress, support systems can offer perspective, comfort, and practical aid.

For those dealing with anxiety, depression, grief, or other mental health issues, leaning on trusted connections provides motivation, encouragement, and a sense of connection. Regular social interaction improves mood, reduces feelings of isolation, and builds resilience to everyday stressors.

Consistently nurturing relationships leads to increased emotional adaptability and determination. Whether through community involvement, close friendships, or professional help, cultivating a strong support network enhances your ability to cope with challenges and promotes overall well-being.

Practice Gratitude for Emotional Balance

Gratitude practice is the intentional act of recognizing and appreciating the positive aspects of life, whether big or small. It involves shifting attention from what is lacking to what is present, harnessing a mindset rooted in thankfulness. Research consistently shows that individuals who practice gratitude experience improved mental health, increased resilience, and greater overall well-being.

By actively acknowledging the good in life, people can nurture a more optimistic outlook. Gratitude strengthens emotional resilience, helping individuals better cope with stress and adversity. There are many ways to practice gratitude, including verbal or written appreciation, reflecting on meaningful experiences, keeping a gratitude journal, and engaging in mindfulness or gratitude meditation. Expressing appreciation might involve saying phrases like, "Thank you," "I appreciate you," or "I'm grateful you're in my life," or writing a thoughtful note to someone. These simple acts can brighten someone's day and often lift the spirit of the person offering gratitude as well.

Reflecting on positive experiences such as past successes, joyful moments, or meaningful connections offers another way to deepen gratitude. Keeping a gratitude journal, where one regularly writes down things they're thankful for, reinforces this mindset. Meditation can also play a valuable role, especially during challenging times. Mindfulness and gratitude meditation help people stay grounded in the present and appreciate the simple things in life. Beginning the day with a positive affirmation, such as declaring, "Today will be a great day no matter what," sets a constructive tone for the day.

Gratitude can be integrated into different seasons of life. Whether during stress, anxiety, burnout, low motivation, or transitions, gratitude provides grounding and emotional clarity. Practicing gratitude in moments of tension or conflict helps shift focus from problems to possibilities, supporting conflict resolution and emotional regulation. It can help individuals reconnect with their purpose by reflecting on past accomplishments and joys, especially during periods of apathy or burnout.

In times of uncertainty or change, gratitude provides reassurance by highlighting stability and support systems. Expressing appreciation strengthens relationships, deepens connection, and fosters mutual respect. Over time, the regular practice of gratitude contributes to a lasting sense of happiness, life satisfaction, and mental clarity.

Whether through journaling, creating a gratitude jar, offering appreciation to others, or engaging in reflective meditation, gratitude is a powerful and accessible tool. It promotes mental, physical, and emotional health. Learning to foster gratitude early in life lays a strong foundation for resilience in the face of stress, anxiety, anger, guilt, or grief. Positive affirmation and daily thankfulness create emotional strength to endure and overcome life's inevitable difficulties.

Self-Compassion and Self-Acceptance

Self-compassion is the practice of treating oneself with love, kindness, patience, understanding, and forgiveness. It creates a foundation for extending compassion to others. Self-compassion means recognizing personal struggles without harsh judgment and embracing imperfection as part of the human experience.

Psychologist Dr. Kristin Neff introduced the concept of self-compassion and identified its three essential components: self-kindness, mindfulness, and shared humanity. Self-kindness involves offering oneself understanding and support in moments of failure. Common humanity acknowledges that everyone suffers and struggles, creating connections instead of isolation. Mindfulness allows for awareness of negative emotions without exaggerating or denying them. This includes fully accepting emotional experiences without judgment.

Practicing self-compassion offers powerful psychological benefits, including reduced anxiety and emotional distress, increased resilience, and improved emotional well-being. It fosters a positive self-image and helps people approach challenges with inner strength rather than self-criticism. Unlike self-esteem, which often relies on external validation, self-compassion provides internal emotional support. Once people learn to validate themselves, they no longer depend on others to define their self-worth. Though external validation may still feel good, it becomes a bonus, not a necessity.

Self-compassion also promotes healthier motivation. People who are kind to themselves are more likely to take risks, learn from failure, and persevere through adversity. They understand that mistakes don't define them. They offer valuable lessons. Many individuals struggle with self-compassion due to societal messages that equate worth with success or perfection. Cultural expectations, media influences, and upbringing can reinforce the belief that love and acceptance must be earned. Self-compassion directly challenges that narrative by affirming that everyone deserves understanding and kindness regardless of accomplishments or perceived failures.

Developing self-compassion takes intention and practice. One of the most effective tools is positive self-talk. Instead of saying, "I always fail," one might say, "I'm learning and growing through this." This simple reframing shifts perspective and builds emotional resilience.

Another method is prioritizing self-care. Engaging in restful, enjoyable activities and practices that nourish the mind and body communicates that one's well-being matters. Self-care is not selfish. It is a fundamental part of self-compassion. Whether through meditation, movement, social connection, or stillness, acts of self-care reinforce self-worth.

Mindfulness meditation is a powerful tool in this process. It helps individuals observe thoughts and emotions with acceptance, preventing negative self-talk from spiraling—simple practices like body scans, grounding techniques, or progressive muscle relaxation support emotional regulation and self-awareness.

Journaling is another valuable approach. Writing about personal experiences from a place of compassion can help reframe challenges and process emotions. A self-compassion journal, where one records kind thoughts, reflections, and personal growth, serves as a reminder of inherent value and strength.

Seeking professional support through therapy or structured programs can also nurture self-compassion. Approaches like Cognitive Behavioral Therapy (CBT), Dialectical Behavior Therapy (DBT), and Acceptance and Commitment Therapy (ACT) often integrate self-compassion as a cornerstone of emotional healing. Self-compassion is especially vital during times of failure or disappointment—many turn to harsh self-judgment in such moments, which undermines motivation and confidence. Responding with compassion allows for growth without damage to self-worth. It reframes failure as an opportunity, not a verdict.

In moments of deep emotional distress, grief, fear, anger, anxiety, and self-compassion offers a path to healing. Rather than suppressing emotions or feeling guilty for them, acknowledging and accepting pain with tenderness helps soothe the inner struggle. Self-compassion supports personal transformation by reducing fear of change or failure. It creates emotional safety for setting new goals, making hard decisions, or taking brave steps forward. When practiced consistently, self-compassion becomes an empowering mindset.

It also helps combat self-doubt and comparison. In a world driven by appearances and perfection, self-compassion reminds individuals that everyone experiences insecurities. Embracing this shared humanity allows for a healthier, more realistic self-view. Self-compassion is essential in relationships. It helps individuals set boundaries, communicate authentically, and show empathy to others.

When people treat themselves with love and respect, they are better equipped to offer the same to those around them, fostering more meaningful, supportive connections. Ultimately, self-compassion is vital to emotional resilience, mental health, and personal growth. It empowers individuals to move through life with grace, courage, and a strong sense of self-worth. Being kind to oneself is not a weakness; it is one of the most potent forms of strength.

While the tools we've covered so far provide a solid foundation for emotional management, there are always new techniques and strategies to deepen our resilience and emotional agility. In this chapter, we will expand on the toolkit, introducing additional methods that can complement and strengthen the practices you've already learned. From grounding techniques to body-centered practices, these tools will help you respond to emotions with greater insight, flexibility, and control, empowering you to face life's challenges with confidence and composure.

Interactive Reflection: Your Emotional First-Aid Kit

Consider this chapter your emotional toolbox, and now it's time to personalize it.

Draw two columns in your journal. Label one "Tools I Use Often" and the other "Tools I'd Like to Explore."

Revisit the tools covered, such as, mindfulness, journaling, movement, nutrition, sleep, social connection, gratitude, self-compassion. Reflect honestly:

- Which of these already help me?

- Which ones feel unfamiliar or underused, but worth trying?

Self-regulation isn't about perfection. It's about preparation. Build your toolbox now, so you're not reaching in the dark when storms arrive.

Chapter 6
Additional Tools for Coping with Emotions

"Nature, music, and connection to spirit are the ancestral tools we forget we need. But they never stopped working."

- Dr. C. A. Castillo

The journey to emotional resilience is ongoing, and as we continue to build our emotional toolkit, it's important to recognize that there's no one-size-fits-all approach. In this chapter, we'll explore additional tools for coping with emotions that can provide new perspectives and deeper levels of healing. From creative expression to body-based practices, these strategies will empower you to enhance emotional regulation, boost your resilience, and tap into your inner strength when facing life's inevitable emotional ups and downs. With each new tool, you'll be better equipped to navigate your emotional landscape with confidence.

Setting and Maintaining Healthy Boundaries

Setting boundaries means defining clear limits to protect your mental, emotional, and physical well-being. Boundaries communicate what is acceptable and unacceptable behavior in both personal and professional relationships. When practiced consistently, they foster mutual respect, enhance communication, and preserve a healthy sense of self.

Without boundaries, people may experience burnout, frustration, or emotional distress from overextending themselves. While many people think of a boundary simply as a line or limit, it's essential to recognize that a functional boundary has three parts:

1. The boundary itself is the limit being set.

2. The consequence or reward: what happens if the boundary is violated or respected?

3. The execution follows through with the consequence or reward.

Execution is often the most challenging part. Yet, it is essential. Without follow-through, a boundary is merely a suggestion, not a limit. If someone is allowed to cross a boundary without consequence, they're likely to do so again.

It's also crucial that the consequence or reward is meaningful to the person receiving it. For instance, a parent may set a boundary with their children: if they respect it, they're rewarded with ice cream, two extra scoops even. If they violate it, they lose three hours of game time. The key is consistent follow-through. Boundaries mean little if not upheld.

There are several types of boundaries:

- Time boundaries: help manage commitments and avoid overextension.

- Emotional boundaries: protect one's feelings and energy.

- Physical boundaries involve personal space and physical touch.

- Relational boundaries govern expectations within family, romantic, professional, or social dynamics.

Boundaries are a form of self-care. They allow people to prioritize their needs without guilt, creating a balance between giving and receiving. Without them, one might feel disrespected, taken for granted, or emotionally exhausted. Learning to set and enforce boundaries is key to preserving emotional and mental well-being.

Importantly, boundaries are not about shutting others out. They're about fostering mutual respect and protecting personal integrity. People who struggle with boundary-setting often fear conflict or rejection. But clearly communicating your limits calmly and assertively helps create stronger, healthier relationships.

Effective boundaries require:

- Self-awareness: recognizing what causes stress or discomfort.

- Clear communication: Use "I" statements like, "I feel overwhelmed when the house is messy" or "I need time for myself."

- Consistency: ensuring consequences are applied when boundaries are crossed.

Consistency builds trust. If you repeatedly allow your boundaries to be ignored, others may not take them seriously. For example, if someone invades your personal space and you say nothing, they're likely to continue. But if you set the limit and follow through with action, you reinforce the importance of that boundary.

Self-compassion is also vital. Boundaries should serve your well-being and not be compromised for fear of upsetting others. It's okay to say "no" without guilt. People may push back against limits, but standing firm protects your emotional space.

Boundaries offer a way to maintain personal power. They protect your time, energy, and peace of mind. Whether you're dealing with friendships, family dynamics, romantic partnerships, or professional environments, clearly identifying, communicating, and enforcing boundaries leads to more respectful and fulfilling connections. You should consider setting boundaries whenever you feel disrespected, overwhelmed, or emotionally drained. For instance, if a friend frequently demands your time without reciprocating support, it's reasonable to set limits around your availability.

Boundaries support professionalism and work-life balance in the workplace. If a colleague expects you to answer late-night calls, you might say, "I'm unavailable after 6 p.m., but I'll respond during office hours." Requesting emails over spontaneous calls is another way to manage work stress.

Clear emotional and physical boundaries also benefit romantic relationships. If a partner repeatedly dismisses your feelings or disregards your space, setting a firm limit helps establish mutual respect. Family boundaries are often the hardest to set but equally important, especially when dealing with criticism, guilt, or overstepping. If a relative constantly pressures you about personal choices, it's okay to say, "I'm not comfortable discussing this," redirect the conversation or limit the interaction.

Ultimately, boundaries are an essential tool for emotional resilience. They're not walls but bridges that help you stay connected to others without losing yourself. By honoring your limits, you protect your peace and create room for healthier, more meaningful relationships.

Engaging in Creative Outlets (Art, Writing, Music, etc.)

Creative outlets are activities that allow individuals to express their thoughts, emotions, and ideas in a meaningful, often artistic way. These outlets can take many forms, including writing, painting, listening to music, singing, dancing, photography, cooking, traveling, fishing, golfing, gardening, or even physical activities like sports and yoga. They provide a powerful means of channeling emotions, reducing stress and anxiety, and promoting personal growth.

In today's fast-paced world, people turn to creative outlets to escape daily pressures and reconnect with themselves. These activities offer space for self-exploration and skill development. Whether pursued professionally or as a hobby, creative outlets can bring a sense of purpose, calm, and fulfillment, especially during times of emotional strain.

Engaging in creativity is profoundly beneficial for mental and emotional well-being. Research shows that activities like painting or playing a musical instrument can help reduce anxiety, increase concentration, and elevate mood. The process of creation becomes a safe container to release pent-up emotions. Rather than suppressing feelings, individuals can process and make sense of them through creative expression, leading to healing and deeper self-awareness.

Creative outlets also nurture critical thinking and problem-solving skills. When people engage in a creative process, they often view challenges from new angles and explore unconventional solutions. This kind of thinking enhances adaptability and innovation, traits that are beneficial in both personal and professional life. Creativity, after all, isn't confined to the arts; it informs science, technology, business, and everyday decisions.

Beyond personal benefits, creative outlets can foster meaningful social connections. Participating in group activities like a writing circle, music ensemble, or painting class allows individuals to share their passions with others, gain feedback, and grow together. These experiences build community and offer a sense of belonging.

Encouraging children to explore creative interests early in life helps them connect with their passions and strengths. When nurtured, these interests can evolve into fulfilling careers or lifelong hobbies. Supporting children in this way lays the groundwork for confidence, resilience, and self-expression.

Ultimately, creative outlets are potent tools for emotional expression, mental wellness, social connection, and personal exploration. They help individuals navigate life's challenges with more balance, clarity, and joy. To fully benefit from a creative outlet, it's essential to find an activity that resonates personally. This process involves exploration and openness, as well as trying things like journaling, painting, music-making, or photography to see what brings joy and peace. The key is to choose something that feels natural and enjoyable, not forced or stressful.

Once identified, setting aside intentional time for creative engagement is crucial. While many feel too busy for creative pursuits, even a few minutes a day can have a lasting impact. Building a routine like writing for 15 minutes in the morning or sketching during lunch breaks can help cultivate consistency and reinforce the habit.

An essential part of the creative journey is embracing imperfection. The goal isn't to produce a masterpiece. It's to express yourself authentically. Many people hold back creatively due to fear of failure or judgment. But creativity is about growth, not perfection.

Allowing room for mistakes invites playfulness, exploration, and freedom.

Creativity can also be woven into daily life through small, intentional acts: listening to music while cooking, doodling in a notebook during meetings, or taking spontaneous photographs during walks. These simple practices keep creative energy flowing without requiring drastic lifestyle changes. Sharing creative work with others, whether through social media, a local club, or a casual performance, can be incredibly fulfilling. It provides encouragement, inspiration, and fresh perspectives. The act of sharing helps strengthen confidence and enriches the creative experience.

Creative outlets are especially valuable during times of stress or emotional difficulty. In moments of overwhelm, painting, journaling, playing music, or other forms of creative expression can offer soothing relief. These outlets provide healthy alternatives to harmful coping mechanisms and allow emotions to be processed in a safe, meaningful way.

They're also helpful during moments of inspiration. Keeping a notebook, sketchpad, or voice recorder nearby helps capture spontaneous ideas and emotions as they arise. Acting on inspiration in the moment often leads to more genuine and enjoyable creative experiences.

Engaging in creative activity can refresh the mind during times of mental block or problem-solving fatigue. Many breakthroughs occur when the brain is relaxed and diverted. Taking a creative break often leads to renewed clarity and innovative thinking.

During self-reflection or periods of personal growth, creative outlets offer a mirror to explore inner experiences. Writing about past challenges, building a vision board, or composing music based on personal journeys can bring insight, healing, and direction. Through creativity, individuals gain a deeper understanding of themselves.

And sometimes, creativity should simply be fun. Not every creative act needs a purpose or goal. Dancing alone in your room, doodling on napkins, or singing in the shower just for the joy of it is enough. These small moments of spontaneous expression contribute to overall happiness and life satisfaction.

In the end, creative outlets are not luxuries; they are lifelines. They remind us of who we are, help us heal, and bring beauty into our lives in ways both big and small. No matter the form it takes, finding and engaging with your creative outlet can be a transformative experience.

Connecting with Nature for Mental Restoration

Connecting with nature is a powerful and accessible way to enhance mental, emotional, and physical well-being. Whether it's a walk through the woods, time spent near a body of water, or simply sitting in a backyard garden, immersing oneself in a natural environment allows for peace, calm, and deep restoration.

Nature offers a unique opportunity to unplug from daily stressors and experience a mental reset. The sound of ocean waves, birdsong, rustling leaves, and the sight of wide-open landscapes create a soothing atmosphere that encourages relaxation and mindfulness. Spending time in nature has been scientifically proven to reduce symptoms of stress, anxiety, depression, anger, grief, and guilt. Exposure to natural environments lowers cortisol levels, the hormone responsible for stress. Activities such as walking, hiking, or simply sitting by a river can significantly improve mood, enhance clarity, and promote emotional balance.

Nature also nurtures mindfulness. It invites individuals to be present, to observe their surroundings without judgment, and to embrace the moment as it is. This deep presence supports emotional well-being and strengthens self-awareness. Engaging with nature physically offers numerous health benefits. Fresh air, sunlight, and gentle movement can improve cardiovascular health, strengthen the immune system, and increase energy levels. Outdoor activities like swimming, jogging on a trail, or practicing yoga in the open air combine physical exercise with the restorative effects of the natural world. Even brief exposure to nature can promote better sleep and reduce insomnia.

Nature inspires creativity and enhances problem-solving skills. A natural setting often provides mental space for fresh ideas and new perspectives. Writers, artists, and thinkers have long turned to nature for inspiration. Whether brainstorming, sketching, or writing, time spent in nature sparks innovation and mental clarity.

Social connections can also deepen through shared experiences in nature. Group activities like hiking, fishing, camping, boating, or picnicking offer meaningful opportunities to bond with family, friends, or even new acquaintances. Without the usual distractions of technology, these interactions often feel more present and genuine.

Using nature effectively requires intentionality. A straightforward approach is taking daily walks in green spaces, parks, tree-lined streets, or quiet trails. Walking barefoot on grass or sand, also known as grounding, allows the body to absorb Earth's natural energy, which may help reduce stress and support overall wellness.

Mindful observation is another effective way to engage. Listening to birds, watching the movement of water, or noticing the changing colors of leaves fosters stillness and appreciation. Sitting outside for just a few minutes each day can help build a habit of mindfulness. Outdoor hobbies offer yet another path to connection. Gardening, fishing, birdwatching, or photography all combine creativity or productivity with immersion in the natural world. These hobbies provide therapeutic benefits, allowing individuals to unwind, focus, and feel a sense of accomplishment.

Nature also serves as a dynamic learning environment. Schools often incorporate outdoor classrooms and field trips to teach biology, environmental science, and sustainability. People can also develop valuable survival skills like plant identification, fire-making, and natural navigation. The military, for instance, uses nature in training to enhance adaptability and resourcefulness.

For those practicing meditation or relaxation techniques, nature can amplify the experience. Meditating by the ocean, practicing yoga in a park, or doing deep breathing exercises in a quiet forest can deepen relaxation and offer profound emotional relief. During times of stress or emotional distress, stepping into nature can be immediately soothing. Fresh air, silence, and space provide comfort and perspective. Nature is a free and ever-present resource that offers a place to reflect, recharge, and emotionally recalibrate.

When creativity is blocked or focus is lacking, nature can serve as a mental refresh. A short walk outside often clears mental fog and provides a boost in concentration. Many high-performing individuals attribute their breakthrough moments to quiet time spent in nature.

Feelings of fatigue or low energy are also a signal to reconnect with the natural world. Instead of turning to caffeine, stepping outdoors can boost energy levels naturally. Sunlight increases vitamin D, which plays a key role in mood and vitality, while movement improves circulation and the mind-body connection.

Moments of self-reflection or transition are ideal for engaging with nature. Whether facing a significant decision, managing emotions, or seeking clarity, being in nature offers space free from distraction. Solo hikes, beach walks, or time spent in solitude can lead to greater insight and peace.

Finally, nature can elevate celebrations and shared experiences. Outdoor activities like bonfires, picnics, and beach gatherings enrich birthdays, reunions, and anniversaries. These moments, set in natural beauty, often create lasting memories and deeper connections. Whether alone or with others, engaging with nature is a meaningful, restorative practice that supports overall well-being. It offers healing, inspiration, connection, and clarity, reminding us of our place in the larger world and providing the grounding we often need in a fast-paced life.

Catching More Than Pokémon: Building Resilience Through Play and Connection

In an age where screens often divide us, games like Pokémon GO offer a rare and beautiful opportunity to bring people together not just virtually but physically, emotionally, and even spiritually. Pokémon GO is an augmented reality mobile game that encourages players to explore their surroundings in search of virtual creatures called Pokémon. Using GPS and real-world maps, players walk, talk, and interact with both the environment and one another to capture, train, and battle Pokémon. But beyond the thrill of catching a rare or powerful creature, the game unlocks something even more meaningful: human connection.

Families around the world, including mine, have discovered that Pokémon GO is more than just a game; it's a shared adventure. Parents and children walk side by side, laughing, strategizing, and celebrating small victories as a team. Resilience often takes root in these moments when the rain begins to fall, and they keep going when someone misses a catch, and the others cheer them on to try again. The game becomes a platform for teaching patience, perseverance, and teamwork. Instead of being isolated behind individual screens, families bond by moving, exploring, and problem-solving together in real time.

One of the game's most potent qualities is its ability to dissolve social boundaries. At community events, people from all walks of life, including Black, White, Latino, Asian, Indigenous, and more, gather with a shared goal. There are no political debates, no cultural barriers, no social hierarchies. You'll see a grandmother cheering on a teenager as they both try to catch a rare legendary Pokémon or a group of strangers high-fiving when someone lands a shiny. In these moments, unity overrides division. It reminds us of what we all share: the desire for connection, joy, and collective celebration.

This spirit of collaboration teaches families an essential truth about resilience: we are stronger when we move forward together. When one player struggles, the community lifts them. When someone achieves a milestone, everyone celebrates. These values of encouragement, teamwork, and joy through shared experience are closely tied to mental and emotional resilience. The simple act of showing up together, walking side by side, and supporting one another, even through something as lighthearted as a mobile game, creates ripples that strengthen emotional bonds within families and communities.

In a world often overshadowed by division, Pokémon GO offers a hopeful glimpse of what's possible when we choose unity, connection, and mutual support. Resilience isn't forged in isolation; it is built-in laughter, steps taken together, shared goals, and those moments when we choose connection over conflict. When families engage in games like this, they're not just catching Pokémon. They're catching memories, strengthening relationships, and nurturing the kind of inner strength that helps them weather life's storms. Special thanks to our Lithia, Florida Pokémon Go ambassador (GodivaDeb) and team, Where our meeting is at Fish Hawk Sports Complex, for welcoming my family and me into the family.

Breathing Exercises for Emotional Regulation

Breathing exercises are intentional techniques that promote physical, mental, and emotional well-being by regulating the breath. Through conscious control of inhalation and exhalation, these exercises help calm the nervous system, enhance oxygen flow, and foster relaxation. Practiced for centuries across cultures, especially in yoga, meditation, and mindfulness, breathwork has proven to be a powerful tool for emotional regulation and stress relief.

One of the most notable benefits of breathing exercises is their ability to activate the parasympathetic nervous system, which encourages the body to relax and recover. Techniques like diaphragmatic Breathing and box breathing promote slower, deeper breaths that naturally lower heart rate and blood pressure. As a result, breathwork is an effective method for managing anxiety, panic attacks, and even chronic pain.

Beyond emotional balance, breathing techniques improve respiratory health. Individuals with asthma or chronic obstructive pulmonary disease (COPD) often use these methods to strengthen lung capacity and improve oxygen intake. Athletes, too, benefit from breath control, which enhances endurance and boosts physical performance.

The mental health benefits are equally profound. Breath-based practices help reduce intrusive thoughts, foster mindfulness, and sharpen focus. Methods like alternate nostril breathing and 4-7-8

Breathing are especially helpful in calming the mind and easing emotional distress.

Breathing exercises are especially appealing because they are simple and accessible. They require no special equipment and can be practiced anytime, anywhere. Whether the goal is to reduce stress, improve sleep, or enhance physical performance, integrating breathwork into daily life offers lasting benefits.

Techniques and How to Practice Them

Choosing the proper breathing technique depends on your specific needs:

- Diaphragmatic Breathing (for relaxation): Sit or lie down comfortably. Place one hand on your stomach and the other on your chest. Inhale slowly through your nose, allowing your stomach to rise. Exhale through your mouth, letting your stomach fall. This method promotes full oxygen exchange and calms the body.

- Box Breathing (for focus and control): Inhale for four seconds, hold, exhale, and hold again for four seconds. Repeat the cycle. Popular among athletes and military personnel, this technique helps maintain composure under pressure.

- 4-7-8 Breathing (for anxiety and panic): Inhale through the nose for four seconds, hold for seven seconds, and exhale slowly through the mouth for eight seconds. This technique slows the heart rate and eases the nervous system.

- Alternate Nostril Breathing (for balance and clarity): Close your right nostril with your thumb and inhale through the left nostril. Then close your left nostril and exhale through the right. Alternate nostrils with each breath. This technique is commonly used in yoga to balance energy and focus the mind.

Consistency is essential. Even just a few minutes of daily practice can lead to significant improvements. Ideally, perform these exercises in a quiet, comfortable space free of distractions to maximize their calming effects.

When to Use Breathing Exercises

- During Stressful Moments: When experiencing anxiety or heightened tension, deep Breathing can calm the nervous system and reduce the fight-or-flight response.

- Before Sleep: Breathwork, especially 4-7-8 or diaphragmatic Breathing, can ease racing thoughts and prepare the body for rest.

- During Physical Activity: Athletes often synchronize breathing with movement to improve stamina and performance. Rhythmic Breathing, for example, is common among runners.

- In Emotional Situations: Taking a few deep breaths in moments of anger or frustration allows for reflection before reaction, promoting better emotional control.

- As part of a Mindfulness Routine, incorporating breathwork into daily meditation enhances self-awareness, builds resilience, and nurtures emotional balance.

The Power of Music and Audiobooks for Resilience, Grit, and Well-being

Music and audiobooks are potent tools for enhancing emotional resilience, mental toughness, and overall well-being. Music uplifts, motivates, and soothes the mind, while audiobooks offer wisdom, inspiration, and perspective. Together, they can support focus, reduce stress, and build inner strength. Music influences our emotions by stimulating neural pathways linked to motivation and relaxation. Energetic, rhythmic music can boost mood and drive while calming melodies reduce tension and aid in emotional regulation. Audiobooks complement this by delivering real-life stories, expert insights, and motivational messages that foster perseverance and growth.

During challenging times, both music and audiobooks offer comfort and strength. A well-chosen song can bring relief or a sense of connection, while a compelling audiobook can provide strategies for coping with adversity. These resources help reframe difficult situations and encourage a forward-thinking mindset.

They're also valuable in times of achievement. Music enhances feelings of joy and celebration, reinforcing a sense of progress. Audiobooks, especially those focused on personal development, support discipline and cultivate grit traits essential for sustained success. Ultimately, weaving music and audiobooks into your daily routine can enhance emotional resilience and mental clarity. Whether you're looking for motivation, relaxation, or inspiration, audio engagement offers a consistent and effective way to nurture a strong, balanced mind.

Volunteering and Helping Others as a Coping Mechanism

Volunteering or helping others involves selflessly offering time, energy, or resources to support individuals, communities, or causes in need. Rooted in generosity and compassion, it's a powerful way to make a positive impact without expecting financial or material rewards. Whether it's assisting at shelters, mentoring youth, cleaning the environment, or simply offering emotional support, volunteering fosters unity and social responsibility.

Helping others isn't limited to formal volunteer work. Everyday acts of kindness like holding the door, donating unused clothes, or offering a listening ear can make a real difference. Even small gestures can uplift someone's day, proving that volunteering doesn't require a grand effort. The heart of it lies in intentional acts that support others' well-being. Beyond benefiting those on the receiving end, volunteering also supports the volunteer's mental and emotional health. Research shows that helping others can reduce stress, enhance mood, and boost overall life satisfaction. It creates a sense of purpose, fulfillment, and connection, strengthening both emotional resilience and core values.

Volunteering also fosters social bonds and strengthens communities. It brings people together from diverse backgrounds and offers opportunities to learn new skills, build networks, and contribute to a shared purpose. Many find that these experiences lead to personal and professional growth, enhancing communication, leadership, and problem-solving abilities.

Ultimately, helping others is a profound human instinct, one that promotes compassion, connection, and growth. Whether through structured programs or small daily actions, the act of giving creates a ripple effect. It inspires others, nurtures empathy, and contributes to a more caring world.

How to Implement Volunteering in Daily Life

Volunteering can be tailored to your skills, passions, and availability. Start by identifying causes that resonate personally. Whether it's supporting older people, tutoring students, or joining a local clean-up initiative, aligning with your interests ensures a more profound commitment and impact. Doing some research into local organizations or needs can also help you find a meaningful fit.

You can also integrate volunteering into your everyday life. Simple actions like helping a neighbor with groceries or supporting a colleague don't take much time but go a long way in building a culture of compassion. The key is to stay mindful and respond when you see someone struggling or needing help.

Formal volunteering opportunities offer more structure. Many nonprofits, community centers, and charities welcome support in roles ranging from admin work to hands-on service. Some companies also support corporate volunteer initiatives, encouraging employees to give back during work hours promoting empathy and team spirit.

Another powerful approach is to offer your professional skills. A lawyer can provide pro bono services, a teacher can tutor underserved students, and a healthcare worker can assist in free clinics. When you match your expertise with a need, your contribution becomes even more impactful and sustainable.

At its core, volunteering is most effective when done consistently and intentionally. Whether through organized efforts or spontaneous kindness, every act matters. Each one strengthens your sense of purpose while helping to create a more connected and compassionate society.

When to Help Others

While volunteering is always valuable, certain times in life amplify its importance. During crises such as natural disasters, pandemics, or economic hardship, volunteering can offer vital support. Whether it is providing food, shelter, or emotional aid, these actions help communities rebuild and heal.

Major life transitions are also ideal times to give back. Moving to a new city, starting retirement, or facing personal challenges can feel disorienting. Volunteering offers structure, connection, and meaning during these periods, helping to ground you and shift your focus outward. Seasonal opportunities like during the holidays or back-to-school periods also present a chance to serve. These times can be especially tough for individuals facing loneliness or financial strain.

Donating gifts, preparing meals, or offering time can bring light to someone's life when they need it most. Equally important are the everyday moments when someone close to you is struggling emotionally, physically, or mentally. Being present, checking in, or offering support in small ways can make a lasting impact.

The best time to help others is always now. Every moment presents a chance to be kind, supportive, and engaged in creating a better world.

Seeking Professional Help When Needed

Seeking professional help is a vital step in maintaining your mental, emotional, and physical well-being. Life can be overwhelming, and reaching out for support doesn't signal weakness. It shows strength and self-awareness. Whether you're navigating anxiety, depression, trauma, or relationship challenges, professional guidance provides tools and insight to manage these issues effectively.

One key benefit of professional support is access to trained expertise. Therapists, counselors, and medical practitioners use evidence-based methods to help individuals heal and grow. They offer a safe, confidential space where you can speak freely without fear of judgment, a crucial factor in the healing process.

Delaying professional help can worsen symptoms, strain relationships, and affect overall health. Emotional distress often manifests physically as fatigue, headaches, or a weakened immune system. Early intervention can prevent further deterioration and promote long-term wellness.

There are many types of support available. Depending on your needs, you might turn to psychologists, psychiatrists, social workers, or general practitioners. In addition, support groups, hotlines, and online therapy platforms offer accessible entry points to care.

Choosing to seek help is an act of self-care. It shows a willingness to invest in your well-being and embrace growth. We all face challenges, and no one has to do it alone. Professional guidance can provide clarity, direction, and healing.

How to Use Professional Help Effectively

To get the most out of professional support, it's essential to approach it with openness and intention. Start by identifying the type of help you need and researching qualified professionals who align with your values and comfort level. Trust is foundational, so it's essential to find someone you feel safe with.

Once in the process, be honest and transparent. Professionals rely on accurate information to tailor effective strategies. While it may feel uncomfortable at first, expressing your thoughts and feelings openly allows for real progress.

Consistency matters. Attending sessions regularly, following through on treatment plans, and practicing recommended strategies outside of sessions are crucial for lasting change. Growth takes time, so be patient with yourself and trust the process.

It's also essential to actively apply the coping tools provided, whether journaling, mindfulness, boundary-setting, or communication skills. Transformation happens not just in sessions but in daily life.

Finally, check in with yourself. If something isn't working, whether it's the approach or the practitioner, it's okay to reassess and try a different path. Healing is a personal journey, and it's okay to seek what truly serves you. Professional help isn't a last resort; it's a resource. And when used with courage, honesty, and persistence, it becomes a powerful ally in your journey toward well-being.

While we've explored a variety of tools to cope with emotions, it's important to see how these strategies can be applied in real life. In this chapter, we turn to Dominique's story, someone who has faced her own emotional challenges and found healing through the tools we've discussed. Her journey of resilience, recovery, and self-discovery will provide powerful insights into how these tools can transform the way we handle emotions, turning adversity into an opportunity for growth. Amina's experience is a testament to the power of applying what we've learned, and her story will inspire you to take the next step in your own healing journey.

Interactive Reflection: Boundary Mapping

Boundaries are not walls. They are doors with locks, handles, and welcome mats. It should be your choice who enters and how.

On a blank page, draw three concentric circles.

- In the center: people and situations that nourish and support you.

- In the middle: those that require discernment or conditional access.

- On the outer ring: what or who must remain at a distance for your peace.

This exercise isn't about judgment, it's about alignment. Your energy is sacred. Protect it intentionally.

Chapter 7
Dominique's Use of Tools for Healing

"Her strength didn't come from surviving, it came from choosing to live fully, loved openly, and heal intentionally."

- Dr. C. A. Castillo

In this chapter, we take a closer look at Dominique's journey, a powerful example of how the tools we've explored can lead to true healing. Dominique has faced significant emotional struggles, yet through the intentional use of mindfulness, emotional regulation techniques, and the support of her own resilience, she has transformed her life. Her story is not just about overcoming adversity but about using the very tools we've discussed to reconnect with herself, heal from past wounds, and build a future rooted in strength and authenticity. Dominique's path to healing will inspire you to embrace the tools at your disposal, knowing that true growth lies in their application.

Mindfulness and Meditation

Dominique learned early on that life's struggles wouldn't vanish, but her response to them could shape her reality. Living between cultures and expectations, she turned to mindfulness and meditation to reclaim her sense of control. She began with simple moments: closing her eyes for a few minutes each morning, grounding herself before the day began.

Over time, she discovered guided meditations online that taught her to focus on her breath, acknowledge emotions without judgment, and release the pain that no longer served her. Instead of being consumed by the past, she developed an inner sanctuary, a space of calm amid the chaos.

Meditation became her tool for resilience. It gave her the ability to pause before reacting. When the pressure of being an outsider in a new home felt overwhelming, she breathed through the discomfort instead of letting it dictate her behavior. She visualized herself moving through obstacles, reinforcing the belief that she could shape her future. This practice helped her sit with difficult emotions without shutting down, growing more adaptive and emotionally aware.

Through mindfulness, Dominique began to rewrite her story. She no longer saw herself as abandoned or unwanted but as someone on a unique path, one that demanded strength and growth. During meditation, she whispered affirmations to herself: I am strong. I am worthy. I am enough. Over time, these words took root. They became her truth. And with them, her resilience deepened.

Journaling

Dominique often felt invisible during her childhood, but journaling gave her a voice. At first, her writing came out in jagged and raw letters to people who had left unsent apologies and unanswered questions. She poured her emotions onto the page, chronicling the journey from a quiet village to the overwhelming streets of a new country.

This process helped her make sense of her pain. Rather than letting it fester within, she gave it shape and release. Writing also allowed her to process her ambitions and setbacks. When she felt lost, she listed the challenges she had already overcome. When she doubted herself, she recorded small victories: a good grade, a new friend, a moment of courage.

Journaling became a ritual of self-reflection and growth. It gave her something tangible: a record of her transformation. More importantly, it gave her control over her narrative. She was no longer defined by what had happened to her. Through her writing, she envisioned what could be.

She began to draft her dreams of who she wanted to become and what she wanted to achieve. The simple act of putting pen to paper became a lifeline. It turned pain into purpose and fear into fuel.

Exercise

At first, Dominique saw exercise as a necessity, not a tool for healing. She'd walked everywhere as a child in her village. In the United States, she kept moving, this time with purpose. Running cleared her mind. Stretching eased the tension in her body. Training became a reflection of the strength she was building from within.

The exercise taught her perseverance. When she first started running, a single mile felt impossible, but she refused to give up. Day by day, step by step, she built endurance. That same persistence showed up in every other area of her life: academics, relationships, and goals.

Physical movement mirrored mental resilience. When old memories resurfaced or life felt too heavy, she didn't spiral. She ran. She lifted. She moved. Each step and rep reminded her that she was strong and in control. Her body became a testament to everything she had survived and everything she was becoming.

Healthy Nutrition

For Dominique, food wasn't just fuel. It became an expression of care, discipline, and identity. Growing up, meals were sometimes uncertain, but they were always made with love. In her new life, she began to understand the connection between what she ate and how she felt.

She started making intentional choices, eating for energy, mental clarity, and emotional balance. She avoided excess sugar when she needed to focus, chose protein before exams, and kept hydrated to stay sharp. Nutrition became an extension of the self-discipline she was developing in every area of life.

Food also reconnected her to her roots. She began cooking meals from her childhood, blending the comfort of the past with the tools of her present. Preparing food became a sacred act and honoring where she came from and where she was headed. By nourishing her body, she reinforced a more profound belief: she was worthy of strength, care, and vitality.

Adequate Sleep

For much of her life, sleep had been an afterthought sacrificed for survival. As a child, she stayed up late studying by candlelight. As a teenager, she lay awake, haunted by questions of identity and belonging. But eventually, Dominique realized that rest wasn't a luxury. It was a necessity.

Prioritizing sleep became a form of self-respect. She built a nighttime routine with calming rituals, trading exhaustion for restoration. She no longer glorified sleepless nights. Instead, she embraced rest as preparation for learning, for growth, for the challenges ahead.

More than anything, sleep became a space for healing. In her dreams, she revisited the parts of herself, still seeking comfort. She released the anxieties that once kept her up, trusting that rest would bring renewal. She began to see that resilience wasn't just about pushing through pain; it was about preserving her strength for the journey ahead.

Social Support: Strength in Community

In a world where Dominique often felt like an outsider, she discovered that resilience wasn't just about pushing through hardships alone; it was also about leaning on others. She found solace in friendships that became her chosen family, people who didn't see her as a girl weighed down by her past but as someone with a future worth believing in.

In high school, Dominique met Ms. Thompson, a teacher who recognized her potential and encouraged her to apply for leadership programs. With each word of support, Dominique felt the heaviness of her isolation lift. She began to understand that strength wasn't rooted solely in independence but in connection.

When she got to college, social support became even more vital. She joined cultural organizations that celebrated her roots, connecting with peers who shared similar stories of displacement and perseverance. Together, they laughed about the challenges of blending two worlds, shared their fears of failure, and helped one another through the struggles of navigating unfamiliar systems. In these relationships, Dominique found validation not just for her ambitions but for the person she was becoming.

Even in adulthood, through the trials of career challenges and personal upheavals, Dominique knew she didn't have to carry the weight alone. She built a circle of support: a mentor who guided her professionally, a best friend who reminded her to rest, and a therapist who helped her unpack the trauma she had carried for years. Through these connections, Dominique realized that true resilience wasn't about enduring silently; it was about knowing when to reach for the hands extended to lift her.

Practicing Gratitude: Finding Light in Darkness

For much of her early life, Dominique focused on survival, always moving forward, afraid to pause and acknowledge what she had. But as she matured, she discovered that resilience wasn't just about weathering the storm; it was about noticing the light that filtered through.

She began a daily habit of writing down three things for which she was grateful. At first, it felt forced. But over time, this small act became a grounding force. She started to notice the quiet triumphs: a warm meal after a difficult day, the laughter of a friend who made her feel at home, and the realization that she was no longer the lost little girl searching for belonging.

By shifting her focus from what was missing to what was present, Dominique lightened the emotional load of her past. Gratitude became her silent protest against despair, a reminder that even in her darkest seasons, there was always something worth holding onto.

When life tested her through a failed exam or the heavy weight of expectation, Dominique returned to her gratitude practice. It reminded her that setbacks were temporary and that her journey was bigger than any single stumble. Gratitude became her lens for resilience, allowing her to reframe struggle and appreciate the strength she had been building along the way.

Self-Compassion: Learning to Be Gentle with Herself

Dominique spent much of her life trying to prove her worth to her family, to society, and to herself. But eventually, she realized that resilience wasn't just about pushing harder; it was also about softening. For years, she had been her own harshest critic, interpreting mistakes as personal failures rather than lessons.

Self-compassion changed that.

She began to shift her inner dialogue. Instead of berating herself for struggling, she started to speak to herself the way she would speak to a friend with empathy, patience, and encouragement. She reminded herself of all she had survived and that it was okay to be tired, to need rest, to ask for help.

Over time, self-compassion became the balm for her inner wounds. She allowed herself to be imperfect, understanding that resilience wasn't about being unbreakable; it was about knowing how to heal when broken. She forgave herself for chasing approval and for the times she put others' needs above her own. Through self-compassion, Dominique came to understand that her value wasn't tied to achievement or productivity but rooted in the truth that she was worthy, just as she was.

Setting Boundaries: Protecting Her Peace

As a child, Dominique learned to shrink herself to accommodate, avoid conflict, and not be a burden. But with time, she came to see that resilience didn't mean carrying every weight. It meant discerning which burdens to release.

Setting boundaries became central to her emotional well-being.

At work, she began to reject unreasonable expectations. She learned to say "no," not in rebellion but in respect for her own capacity. In friendships and relationships, she stopped overextending herself to those who didn't reciprocate her care. Instead, she prioritized connections that left her nourished, not drained.

Dominique's most profound boundaries were internal. She stopped letting guilt shape her decisions, loosened the grip of old expectations, and permitted herself to walk away from what no longer served her. She understood that resilience didn't only mean standing tall; it also meant knowing when to let go. Through boundaries, Dominique reclaimed her peace. She curated a life that honored her emotional safety and affirmed her right to protect it.

Creative Outlets: Healing Through Expression

For years, Dominique carried stories she had never dared to share, memories, emotions, and thoughts that lived silently inside her. But creative expressions became her lifeline. Writing offered a sanctuary where she could explore her past without fear or judgment. Through poetry and storytelling, she wove fragments of her childhood into something tangible, something that gave meaning to her pain.

She also found freedom in movement. Dance became her release, a way to shake off the weight of her history and reconnect with herself. The rhythm reminded her that joy still existed even in the most challenging moments. Art, in all its forms, became a bridge between her past and present, a way to transform suffering into something meaningful and cathartic.

When Dominique began sharing her work, she discovered something powerful: her resilience wasn't just personal; it was universal. People saw themselves in her words. They found comfort in her honesty and strength in her vulnerability. Through creative expression, she turned survival into art, pain into wisdom, and resilience into a story that inspired others to heal, endure, and thrive.

Breathing Exercises: Finding Calm Amidst Chaos

Dominique came to understand that survival wasn't just about pushing through. It was about mastering the mind. The weight of expectations, the ache of displacement, and the pressure to succeed often felt overwhelming. In those quiet, anxious moments, she found refuge in her breath.

At first, it was instinctual, a deep inhale before an exam, a calming breath to ease the ache of missing home. But over time, breathwork became more than a reflex. It became a practice of resilience. She learned diaphragmatic breathing, drawing air deep into her lungs, holding it, then releasing it slowly through pursed lips. This simple ritual grounded her when emotions threatened to take over.

When anxiety struck, when she felt invisible in a crowded room or lost in the uncertainty of her future, she turned to box breathing: inhale for four counts, hold for four, exhale for four, pause for four. The rhythm became her anchor, a quiet rebellion against chaos. As she matured, Dominique added daily meditation for just a few minutes each morning to breathe with intention and settle her mind.

Life remained unpredictable, but breathing gave her clarity and calm. It reminded her that resilience wasn't just about enduring; it was about pausing, recalibrating, and continuing forward. By mastering her breath, she learned to master her emotions and, in turn, her future.

Listening to Music and Audiobooks: Strength in Words and Melodies

From a young age, music was Dominique's haven. Whenever the world felt too loud, she'd slip on her headphones and let the melodies carry her away. Music spoke the language of emotions she hadn't yet learned to articulate. Some lyrics mirrored her loneliness, her longing for connection, and her quiet hope that life would one day be different.

Upbeat rhythms pushed her forward through difficult moments; soft ballads soothed her racing mind. Music became her constant companion, whispering that she wasn't alone.

Later, she discovered audiobooks. What started as a tool to improve her English soon became something more profound. She found herself drawn to memoirs of immigrants, stories of survival, and personal growth. Books like Atomic Habits by James Clear, Start with Why by Simon Sinek, Hurt People, Hurt People by Dr. Wilson, and The Obstacle Is the Way by Ryan Holiday shifted her mindset. Hardship, she learned, wasn't something to run from; it could be transformed into strength.

She created playlists for different moods: one for motivation, another for rest, and another for reflection. Audiobooks guided her through her own challenges, offering wisdom from those who had walked hard paths before her. These small habits became cornerstones of resilience, empowering her to keep going with courage, compassion, and clarity.

Volunteering: Turning Pain into Purpose

Dominique knew what it felt like to be unseen too long for a helping hand that never came. So, when her life gained a sense of stability, she made a promise to be that hand for someone else. She began volunteering at a local shelter, serving meals to people who had even less than she once did. At first, it felt like a simple act of giving back. But as she listened to the stories of the people she served, single mothers escaping violence, teens aged out of foster care, and elders with no one left, she realized that service wasn't just about giving. It was about healing.

Volunteering became her refuge. She mentored young girls and boys from complex backgrounds, helped kids with homework, and offered the encouragement she had once needed herself. She shared her story not as a tragedy but as testimony. Each act of kindness helped her shed the weight of her past.

Through service, Dominique found that strength didn't always look like stoicism. Sometimes, strength meant transforming pain into purpose. Volunteering didn't just change others. It changed her. It reminded her that she was not her wounds but what she chose to build from them.

Seeking Professional Help: Embracing Growth and Healing

For a long time, Dominique believed that resilience meant doing it all on her own. She had survived abandonment, displacement, and loneliness. Surely, she could survive the rest. But even with achievements under her belt, the past still crept into the present, especially in the quiet hours of the night.

A mentor first suggested therapy. She resisted. Asking for help felt like admitting failure. But deep down, she knew that real strength wasn't about pretending to be unbreakable; it was about knowing when to seek support.

The first session was hard. She had challenges trusting. Speaking her truth out loud felt like reopening wounds she had carefully tucked away. But over time, she discovered that therapy wasn't a weakness; it was an act of courage. She unpacked thoughts of suicide, grief, guilt, depression, anxiety, and anger. She permitted herself to feel.

With her therapist, Dominique learned that healing meant facing pain head-on. It meant understanding it, embracing it, and refusing to be defined by it. Therapy taught her how to set boundaries, navigate relationships, and prioritize herself. That decision to ask for help was one of the most transformative choices she ever made. It didn't erase the past, but it helped her rewrite its meaning.

Living Fully: The Art of Resilience

Through breath, Dominique found calm. Through art, she found her voice. Through music and story, she found strength. Through service, she found purpose. Through therapy, she found healing.

She didn't just survive; she learned how to live.

Wellness became a daily practice: mindfulness, journaling, movement, nutrition, and rest. These weren't just self-care habits. They were anchor tools that allowed her to keep rising even when life tried to pull her under.

Dominique's journey wasn't about erasing pain. It was about transforming it, creating a life of meaning, connection, and possibility. Her story became a testament to the quiet power of resilience, not the kind that never breaks but the kind that rebuilds again and again.

Dominique's story highlights the profound impact that emotional tools and resilience can have on an individual's healing process. As we move into the next chapter, we'll reflect on the key lessons learned from her journey and from our exploration of emotional resilience. These lessons are not just theoretical; they are practical and actionable insights that can be applied to our own lives. In the next chapter, we will distill the essential takeaways that will help you build your own path to healing, resilience, and a deeper understanding of your emotional landscape.

Interactive Reflection: Letters Across Time

Dominique's story is one of reclamation: of her voice, her power, her worth. You, too, have such a journey.

Write a short letter to your younger self. What would you say from this place of growth? What comfort, truth, or permission would you offer?

Then write a second letter from your future self, the one who has fully embraced healing. What encouragement does that version of you send back through time?

These letters are more than words. They are bridges. Walk across them.

Chapter 8
Lessons from the Journey

"The most powerful lesson is this: your story, no matter how painful, is sacred. And you are the author."

- Dr. C. A. Castillo

Mental health is a vital component of overall well-being, yet it is often overlooked or misunderstood. When neglected, it can become a silent threat like high blood pressure, diabetes, or carbon monoxide poisoning. While those are primarily physical, suicide often begins with emotional distress that escalates into self-harm.

In a society that constantly demands productivity, resilience, and emotional control, many people struggle to recognize and prioritize their mental health. Stress, trauma, self-doubt, and societal pressure can all contribute to emotional burdens that feel insurmountable. Yet understanding and nurturing our mental health is key to living a balanced, fulfilling life. The lessons in this chapter serve as guideposts to help individuals navigate their emotional and psychological well-being.

Each lesson explores a core aspect of mental health, from the power of thoughts to the importance of boundaries, resilience, and forgiveness. These insights reveal the deep connection between mind and body, showing how our daily habits, awareness, and support systems shape our inner world. By embracing these principles, we take a proactive step toward healing, self-growth, and emotional freedom. Mental health is not a fixed destination, it's a journey. The tools shared here offer a foundation for building a stronger, more resilient mindset.

Physical and Mental Health Are Deeply Connected

The link between physical and mental health is undeniable. Poor physical health can intensify emotional distress, while chronic mental strain can manifest as physical symptoms. To thrive, we must stop treating the body and mind as if they compete. Instead, they should work in harmony.

Exercise is one of the most effective ways to support mental health. Movement stimulates the release of endorphins, natural "feel-good" chemicals that help reduce anxiety, stress, and depression. Even light physical activity such as walking, yoga, or stretching can stabilize mood and promote mental clarity.

Sleep is equally vital. A lack of quality rest can increase irritability, decrease focus, and raise stress levels. Prioritizing sleep hygiene, maintaining consistent bedtime, limiting screen time before bed, and creating a calming sleep environment nurture both mental and physical well-being. Nutrition also plays a key role. A balanced diet rich in fruits, vegetables, lean proteins, and omega-3 fatty acids supports brain function and emotional regulation.

In contrast, a diet high in processed foods, sugar, and caffeine can lead to mood instability, fatigue, and elevated stress. When we take care of the body, we are also caring for the mind. A holistic lifestyle that embraces movement, rest, and nourishment is fundamental to long-term emotional health and happiness.

Mental Health Is Just as Important as Physical Health

Mental health deserves the same attention as physical health, but too often, it's sidelined. People don't hesitate to visit a doctor for a physical ailment, yet many hesitate to seek support for mental struggles. This stigma fuels silence and isolation, reinforcing the false belief that mental health challenges are signs of weakness.

Just as regular checkups, nutrition, and exercise maintain physical health, mental wellness requires consistent care. Practices like therapy, meditation, self-reflection, and journaling help regulate emotions and build resilience. When we actively care for our mental well-being, we make healthier choices, strengthen relationships, and better manage stress.

Workplaces, schools, and communities must treat mental health as a shared priority, not just a personal responsibility. Chronic stress, anxiety, and depression are not only emotional burdens; they can also increase the risk of heart disease and weaken immune function. If we normalize mental health support, more people will seek help, and fewer will suffer alone.

Misinformation remains one of the most significant barriers to progress. Many still view depression as laziness or anxiety as something one should simply "snap out of." In truth, mental health disorders are as real and as complex as physical conditions. They deserve professional treatment, compassionate care, and long-term management.

By promoting open, honest conversations, we remove shame and create safe spaces for healing. Prioritizing mental health doesn't diminish the importance of physical health. It affirms that both are essential to a life of balance and meaning.

Mental Detox Is Essential for Clarity and Calm

In a world saturated with noise, digital alerts and constant updates can emotionally overwhelm our minds and become cluttered. Mental detox is the practice of clearing out this noise. Just as we detox the body from toxins, the mind also needs a reset from negative thoughts, stress, and mental overload.

You may need a mental detox if you find yourself trapped in cycles of overthinking, emotional exhaustion, or information fatigue. These "mental toxins" can cloud judgment and obscure what really matters. Taking time to step back, unplug, and slow down can restore clarity and emotional peace.

Mental detox practices vary, but common ones include meditation, deep breathing, journaling, digital breaks, and time in nature. These activities promote mindfulness, helping us observe our thoughts without judgment and reconnect with ourselves. By scheduling regular mental detoxes, we protect our emotional health. They help clear mental fog, reduce anxiety, and improve focus and creativity.

Over time, these practices strengthen emotional regulation, promote self-awareness, and foster inner calm. Detoxing the mind doesn't require a complete lifestyle overhaul. Even small shifts like a quiet walk, tech-free evenings, or a few minutes of deep breathing can have powerful effects. Consistent mental clarity begins with simple, intentional habits.

Self-awareness is Key to Emotional Stability

Self-awareness is the cornerstone of emotional intelligence. It means understanding your thoughts, emotions, and behaviors and recognizing how they influence your life. When we become aware of our inner world, we gain the power to change it.

Without self-awareness, we may repeat destructive habits, unaware of the patterns driving them. For instance, someone who struggles with anger may not realize their outbursts stem from unresolved fear or shame. By becoming curious about our emotional responses, we uncover the root of our reactions and learn to heal them.

Self-awareness also shapes how we relate to others. Without it, we may project pain onto loved ones, communicate poorly, or misinterpret intentions. When we pause to reflect before reacting, we become more empathetic, grounded, and emotionally available.

Mindfulness is a powerful tool for building self-awareness. It teaches us to observe our thoughts without judgment and gently redirect them. Over time, this builds emotional flexibility and helps us respond rather than react.

Cultivating self-awareness is not about perfection, it's about progress. As we learn more about ourselves, we become better equipped to set boundaries, make aligned choices, and show up authentically in our relationships. The journey inward is the most empowering one we can take.

Resilience Can Be Built Over Time

Resilience is the ability to recover from adversity; it is not an innate trait but a skill that can be developed through experience and intention. Life presents inevitable challenges, from personal loss and failure to unexpected hardships. While these experiences can be overwhelming, resilience allows individuals to adapt, learn, and emerge stronger.

A central pillar of resilience is perspective. Resilient people don't view difficulties as permanent roadblocks but as opportunities for growth. They acknowledge their emotions without allowing setbacks to define them. This mindset shift empowers them to find solutions and hold onto hope during challenging times.

Support systems also play a vital role in building resilience. Trusted friends, family members, or mentors can offer comfort and perspective during hard times. While isolation tends to worsen emotional struggles, meaningful connection promotes healing. Reaching out for help isn't a weakness, it's a strategic step toward resilience.

Another key factor is self-care. Healthy habits like regular exercise, restful sleep, and relaxation techniques help maintain emotional and physical strength. When self-care is prioritized, individuals create a stable foundation for managing life's stressors.

Resilience is a lifelong journey. Each challenge we overcome adds to our emotional toolkit. Through persistence, reflection, and healthy coping strategies, anyone can develop resilience and face life's uncertainties with strength and confidence.

Your Thoughts Shape Your Reality

The way we think directly shapes how we feel, behave, and experience the world. Negative thought patterns can trap us in cycles of anxiety, fear, and self-doubt, while positive and realistic thinking builds resilience and confidence. Realizing that our thoughts hold power gives us the ability to reshape our internal narrative.

Cognitive distortions like catastrophizing, overgeneralizing, or harsh self-criticism can warp reality and amplify stress. For instance, someone who frequently thinks, "I'm a failure," may eventually believe it, regardless of their past achievements. The first step to breaking this pattern is recognizing and challenging such thoughts.

Cognitive reframing is a powerful technique for shifting perspective. It involves replacing negative thoughts with more balanced, constructive alternatives. Instead of thinking, "I'll never get it right," one might reframe it as, "I'm still learning, and every step counts." Over time, this practice fosters confidence and emotional stability.

Mindfulness also helps manage thoughts. By observing our thinking without judgment, we can distance ourselves from negative mental loops. Practices like meditation, deep breathing, or daily affirmations support a calmer, more intentional mindset.

Ultimately, the mind is a tool. With awareness and consistent effort, we can use it to build peace, clarity, and confidence. Changing thought patterns takes time, but the transformation is worth the patience and practice.

Boundaries Are Essential for Mental Wellness

Establishing boundaries is fundamental to emotional well-being and healthy relationships. Many people struggle to say "no" due to guilt, fear of rejection, or societal pressure. Yet without clear boundaries, we risk becoming overextended, resentful, and emotionally depleted.

Boundaries clarify what is acceptable in our personal, professional, and digital lives. They prevent burnout and encourage balance. Saying "no" when necessary protects our time, energy, and emotional health, allowing space for rest and self-care.

A common obstacle to boundary-setting is the fear of being misunderstood or alienating others. But setting limits doesn't damage relationships, it strengthens them. When we communicate our needs with honesty and respect, we invite mutual understanding and reduce resentment.

Boundaries apply in digital spaces, too. The constant connectivity of social media and messaging can lead to overstimulation and fatigue. Setting limits on screen time and online interactions helps preserve mental clarity and peace of mind.

Ultimately, setting boundaries is an act of self-respect. It allows us to protect our well-being and show up more fully in all areas of life. With practice, boundary-setting becomes a powerful tool for emotional stability and authentic living.

Forgiveness and Letting Lead to Freedom

Holding onto resentment, anger, or past pain can be emotionally exhausting. While it may feel justified, unresolved emotions often cause more harm to ourselves than to anyone else. Forgiveness is not about excusing wrongs; it's about freeing ourselves from emotional captivity.

Letting go is a process rooted in self-reflection and healing. Many individuals struggle with forgiveness because they believe it means condoning harmful behavior. But true forgiveness is about loosening the grip the past holds on our present. It's a gift we give ourselves, not a pardon we grant others.

Empathy can help facilitate this process. Recognizing that everyone makes mistakes, even serious ones, can create space for perspective. Understanding that clinging to anger only prolongs our pain allows us to reclaim emotional control.

Self-forgiveness is equally essential. Many people carry deep guilt or shame over past actions, leading to low self-worth and low self-esteem. Accepting our humanity, with all its flaws, opens the door to growth and self-compassion.

Forgiveness doesn't mean forgetting, it means choosing peace over pain. Letting go allows joy, clarity, and renewal to take root. It's through this release that we gain the freedom to move forward, unburdened and empowered.

Mindfulness and Meditation Improve Mental Clarity

Mindfulness and meditation are transformative practices for mental well-being. In today's fast-paced world, it's easy to get caught up in regrets about the past or worries about the future. Mindfulness grounds us in the present, easing stress and promoting emotional clarity.

Meditation, a cornerstone of mindfulness, calms both mind and body. Studies show it reduces anxiety, enhances emotional regulation, and improves focus. Even simple practices like deep breathing, body scans, or guided sessions can offer peace amidst daily tension.

Contrary to popular belief, mindfulness doesn't require hours of stillness. It can be woven into everyday moments while eating, walking, or simply pausing to breathe. The goal isn't to empty the mind but to observe thoughts with compassion and curiosity.

As mindfulness becomes a habit, we begin to respond to stress with extraordinary patience and intention. Rather than reacting impulsively, we learn to pause and reflect. Over time, this practice builds resilience and nurtures a sense of inner calm.

Integrating mindfulness and meditation into daily life supports emotional balance and mental clarity. These practices help us break free from overthinking and develop a healthier relationship with our thoughts. In doing so, we create space for peace, purpose, and presence.

Unresolved Trauma Affects Every Area of Life

Trauma, whether rooted in childhood, relationships, or life-altering events, can leave deep, lasting imprints on mental and emotional well-being. Many people carry unresolved pain without realizing how it shapes their thoughts, behaviors, and emotional patterns. When left unaddressed, trauma can surface in the form of anxiety, depression, trust issues, or self-sabotaging tendencies.

A common reason trauma remains unresolved is the human instinct to suppress painful memories. While avoidance may offer temporary relief, it prevents genuine healing. Unprocessed emotions often resurface in unexpected ways through anger, emotional numbness, or challenges in building and maintaining healthy relationships.

True healing begins with acknowledgment and intentional processing. Trauma-informed therapies, such as Cognitive Behavioral Therapy (CBT) and Eye Movement Desensitization and Reprocessing (EMDR), can help individuals navigate and release painful memories. Talking about one's experiences in a safe, supportive space is a decisive step toward recovery.

Equally crucial to healing is the practice of self-compassion. Many trauma survivors carry misplaced guilt, shame, or feelings of unworthiness. Recognizing that trauma is never the survivor's fault opens the door to self-forgiveness and emotional liberation.

Healing is not a linear path, it's a journey that takes time, patience, and commitment. But facing past wounds, while difficult, leads to emotional freedom, healthier relationships, and a renewed sense of self. Reclaiming one's life begins with the courage to confront what was once too painful to face.

Seeking Help Is a Sign of Strength, Not Weakness

Despite growing awareness, many still hesitate to seek support for mental health challenges. Fear of judgment, stigma, or being seen as "weak" often holds people back. Society has long upheld self-reliance as a virtue, making it harder for individuals to admit when they're struggling. But in truth, recognizing the need for help is a powerful act of strength, self-awareness, and courage.

Professional support through therapy, counseling, or coaching offers tools to navigate complex emotions and life stressors. Mental health professionals provide a safe, nonjudgmental environment, along with insights and coping strategies that friends or family may not be equipped to offer. Therapy helps uncover root causes of distress, whether related to past trauma, anxiety, depression, or chronic stress.

In addition to professional care, leaning on trusted individuals is essential. Sharing struggles with a close friend, mentor, or support group promotes connection and validation. Knowing you're not alone can be incredibly comforting and can reduce the sense of isolation many feel during difficult times.

One of the biggest misconceptions about mental health is the idea that seeking help equates to weakness. But mental health struggles are no different from physical ailments. Just as you would see a doctor for a physical injury, seeking emotional support is vital for healing and growth.

To move forward as a society, we must normalize mental health conversations. By doing so, more people will feel empowered to ask for help without shame. True resilience lies in knowing when to reach out and having the courage to do so. Asking for support is not just an act of survival; it's an act of self-care and, ultimately, a step toward a more grounded and fulfilling life.

Interactive Reflection: Timeline of Growth

Before rushing to the next lesson, pause to witness your path.

Sketch a simple timeline of your life. Highlight 5 key moments that shaped you. Beneath each, answer:

- What happened?

- What did I learn?

- How did I grow?

Growth is rarely loud. Sometimes, it looks like survival. Sometimes, like letting go. But when we see the full picture, we recognize that we are not broken. We are becoming.

Chapter 9
Dominique's Journey to Healing: A Path of Resilience

"Healing isn't linear, it's layered. And each layer brings you closer to the spirit of who you really are."

- Dr. C. A. Castillo

The Mind-Body Connection

Dominique had always treated physical health as a separate aspect of her well-being. She went to the gym regularly, ate balanced meals, and took care of her body. But she never fully acknowledged how deeply her physical and mental health were intertwined.

As stress began to mount from work pressures and personal challenges, she noticed her energy dwindling. Her body felt tense, her muscles ached, and sleep became increasingly elusive. At first, she chalked it up to being busy. But over time, she realized the emotional weight she carried was manifesting in her body. Her stress wasn't just mental, it was physical, too.

Once Dominique recognized this connection, her approach to wellness shifted. She began incorporating practices that soothed both her mind and body: yoga, meditation, deep breathing, and mindful movement. Physical exercise became more than a routine; it became a release valve for her anxiety. Mental relaxation techniques helped her restore balance and clarity.

She discovered that her mental well-being directly influenced her physical health and vice versa. By tending to both, she felt more energized, grounded, and emotionally resilient. Self-care was no longer a luxury and afterthought, it became essential. Dominique realized that resilience wasn't built through sheer willpower alone but through a holistic approach that honored every part of her health. Listening to her body helped her process stress, and in turn, her mental clarity grew. As she treated herself with more care and compassion, she found the strength to face life's challenges with a renewed perspective.

Equal Priorities: Mental Health Matters Too

Dominique had grown up in an environment that praised physical strength and outward success. Mental health, however, was often ignored, brushed aside as weakness, or something to simply "push through." The cultural expectation was to keep going, no matter how you felt inside.

For years, Dominique followed that script. She looked healthy on the outside but was emotionally exhausted on the inside. It wasn't until she reached a breaking point that she realized her emotional well-being had been neglected for far too long.

Understanding that mental health is just as important as physical health marked a significant turning point. She sought out therapy, read self-help books, and began learning how to identify and manage her emotions. She realized that caring for her mind required the same commitment and consistency as caring for her body.

It wasn't an overnight transformation. Changing old habits took time. But little by little, Dominique developed new ones that supported her emotional wellness. She allowed herself to rest, to feel, to process. She learned to extend grace to herself when things got hard.

This shift in mindset transformed how she lived. Mental health was no longer something she addressed. Only when things fell apart did it become a daily practice. She prioritized emotional resilience, self-awareness, and self-compassion. In doing so, she discovered a more profound sense of peace and a more grounded confidence. She learned that true well-being isn't just about appearances, it's about the strength that comes from within.

Mental Detox: Clearing the Clutter

Dominique was no stranger to the chaos of modern life. Between her demanding job, digital overload, and the constant background hum of social media and news, she often felt like her mind was spinning.

She became overwhelmed, anxious, and increasingly disconnected from herself. Focus was fleeting. Peace felt out of reach. Her thoughts raced from one worry to the next, and she realized she was mentally exhausted. That's when she made the conscious decision to embrace a mental detox, a way to declutter her mind and reclaim her sense of calm.

She began small: unplugging from her phone for a few hours each day, limiting exposure to social media, and stepping away from the 24/7 news cycle. Instead, she picked up journaling, spent time in nature, and practiced mindful walking. She started carving out quiet space in her lifetime to be simple.

This intentional slowing down brought clarity. Dominique began to feel lighter, more focused, and far less reactive. Her anxiety eased. Her decision-making improved. Most importantly, she reconnected with herself.

Mental detoxing became a regular part of her routine, not a luxury but a necessity. It allowed her to reset, reflect, and let go of what wasn't serving her. With each mental reset, Dominique strengthened her inner calm and emotional endurance. She found that quieting the noise outside helped her hear her voice more clearly.

The Power of Self-Awareness

Perhaps the most profound change in Dominique's journey came from developing self-awareness. For years, she had been moving through life on autopilot, reacting to situations, ignoring emotional cues, and wondering why specific patterns kept repeating.

Through mindfulness and reflection, Dominique began to notice her triggers. She paid attention to how certain situations made her feel, and instead of pushing emotions down, she explored them. This gave her a sense of clarity she had never experienced before.

With self-awareness came emotional intelligence. Dominique learned to identify when stress was creeping in, when anxiety was taking over, or when she needed rest. Instead of being swept up in emotional waves, she began to respond with intention.

She journaled, meditated, and paused before reacting. These small but consistent acts of mindfulness helped her build emotional stability. When challenges came, and they always did, she met them with a steadier, more grounded presence.

The more Dominique turned into herself, the more resilient she became. Her self-awareness wasn't just a tool for emotional management; it was a compass. It helped her stay aligned with her values, manage relationships with more empathy, and navigate life with a more profound sense of purpose. In learning to listen inwardly, Dominique found her strength. And with it, the grace to grow.

Resilience Is Built Over Time

Dominique once believed that resilience was something you were either born with or without. It seemed like some people just had a natural ability to bounce back while others struggled. Over time, however, she came to see resilience not as an innate trait but as a skill, something that could be grown through intentional effort and consistent practice.

In the early stages of her journey, Dominique faced setbacks that shook her confidence. There were moments she questioned her strength, unsure if she could push through. But she gradually realized that resilience wasn't about avoiding hardship, it was about learning to rise after each fall. It meant choosing to keep moving forward, even when the path felt uncertain.

With this new perspective, Dominique embraced the process of building resilience step by step. She began by setting small, achievable goals and treating each success, no matter how minor, as a sign of progress. When obstacles arose, she stopped viewing them as failures and instead saw them as opportunities to learn and grow. Over time, her emotional stamina strengthened. She bounced back more quickly and adapted more easily to life's ups and downs.

Through this process, Dominique also discovered the importance of grit and the inner determination to keep going despite challenges, missteps, or disappointments. She came to understand that growth wasn't linear. Setbacks didn't mean she was failing; they were just part of the journey. By leaning into resilience and grit, she built a more profound sense of confidence and agency. With every challenge she overcame, she uncovered more of the strength that had always lived inside her.

Your Thoughts Shape Your Reality

As Dominique continued to heal, she became increasingly aware of the power her thoughts held. She began to recognize that the way she interpreted her experiences shaped how she felt and what she believed was possible. For much of her life, she had allowed negative self-talk and limiting beliefs to guide her decisions. When facing challenges, she would immediately think of all the reasons she might fail and, in doing so, often set herself up for precisely that.

Once she understood the link between her thoughts and her reality, she made a conscious decision to shift her mindset. She began challenging the inner critic and replacing self-doubt with more empowering affirmations. Whenever fear crept in, she reminded herself of her past victories and how far she'd already come.

This transformation didn't happen overnight. But gradually, her internal dialogue softened. Her perspective grew more hopeful and forward-looking. She saw that her thoughts could either become roadblocks or stepping stones, and it was up to her to choose which.

This shift in thinking gave Dominique a renewed sense of clarity and purpose. She no longer felt trapped by her old narratives. Instead, she became the author of a new one grounded in self-belief, resilience, and hope. By aligning her thoughts with who she was becoming, she began creating a more empowering and fulfilling reality, one moment at a time.

Forgiveness and Letting Lead to Freedom

One of the most profound lessons Dominique had to learn was the power of forgiveness. For years, she carried the weight of old wounds, betrayals from friends, unresolved conflicts with family, and disappointments in herself. These burdens lingered, quietly shaping her decisions and emotional state. Dominique once believed that holding on to anger and resentment kept her protected. In truth, it only drained her and stalled her growth. She found herself trapped in a cycle of pain that closed her off from the freedom and healing she yearned for.

Through therapy and deep personal reflection, Dominique came to understand that forgiveness and letting go are keys to emotional liberation. She realized forgiveness wasn't about excusing what had happened but about releasing the grip those memories held on her. By forgiving, she reclaimed her emotional power and created space for peace. Even more importantly, she discovered that forgiveness wasn't just outward, it was inward. She had to forgive herself, too. The guilt, shame, and self-judgment she'd been carrying became barriers to growth until she made the courageous choice to let them go.

As Dominique practiced forgiveness, she felt a profound sense of emotional release. The more she released past hurts, the lighter she felt physically, mentally, and spiritually. Forgiveness deepened her resilience by stripping away the emotional weight that once slowed her down. She learned that forgiveness is not a single event but an ongoing journey. It's a choice made daily to release, to heal, to move forward. In embracing this path, Dominique created the space she needed to grow, to hope, and to live more fully.

Growth Through Resilience and Well-Being

Looking back on her journey, Dominique recognized just how far she had come. The lessons she had learned from understanding the mind-body connection to setting healthy boundaries helped her grow resilience and a more profound sense of well-being. Her growth didn't happen overnight; it came through facing hardship and choosing to rise each time she fell. With each challenge, she became more emotionally grounded and self-aware.

Dominique no longer viewed well-being as simply the absence of pain or the pursuit of happiness. To her, it meant creating a balance across her emotional, physical, mental, and spiritual life. Through intentional self-care, mindfulness, and the practice of forgiveness, she learned to nurture herself and her relationships. She no longer dismissed her mental health; it became a priority she actively maintained. This new mindset brought peace and a greater sense of control over her life.

Resilience, once a foreign concept, became part of Dominique's identity. She understood now that it wasn't something you were born with, it was something you could build. When life threw curveballs, she didn't panic. She paused, reflected, and responded with strength, emotional clarity, and hope. The tools she had gathered, emotional regulation, mindfulness, boundary-setting, and self-awareness, became the foundation of her continued growth.

Embracing the Journey of Healing

Dominique's transformation was rooted in profound self-discovery. She learned that mental and physical health were not separate, and by nurturing both, she created lasting well-being. She began to challenge negative thought patterns, replacing them with affirmations that aligned with her growth. Through mental decluttering and releasing old wounds, Dominique found clarity and calm.

Setting boundaries became an act of self-respect. By protecting her energy, she created healthier dynamics in her personal life. Forgiveness also played a critical role. Letting go of past pain didn't erase the past, it freed her from its grip. Through mindfulness and meditation, she found presence and focus, helping her respond to life's stressors with more composure.

As Dominique worked through trauma, she realized how deeply it had affected every area of her life. Facing her pain and allowing herself to be supported helped her move forward with emotional strength. Seeking help wasn't just a turning point, it became a pillar of her wellness. By embracing vulnerability, she accessed the support and tools she needed to heal and grow.

Each insight brought her closer to balance, self-acceptance, and empowerment. Dominique now moves through life with deeper self-awareness and inner strength. She is living proof that healing is possible, that growth is ongoing, and that seeking help is one of the most courageous things we can do.

Awakening

She entered the world with a whispered name,
Dominique, belonging to the Lord all the same.
Yet in their eyes, she bore a stain,
A child of two, yet claimed by none.

Born between worlds, neither here nor there,
A shadow cast in love's despair.
Labeled bastard, left to roam,
Searching for a place called home.

Her heart ached for warmth untold,
Yet met the world so fierce, so cold.
Pain became her closest friend,
A cycle of wounds that would not end.

Anger flared, then grief took hold,
Anxiety whispered, and fear turned cold.
Her mind built walls to keep her safe,
Yet locked her in a lonesome space.

The heart would cry, the mind would chide,
They pulled, they pushed, they would collide.
One sought feeling, the other control,
But neither could make her whole.

She carried the weight of names unkind,
Yet, she sought a light she longed to find.
Through open doors and quiet rooms,
She met herself amid the wounds.

Therapy unraveled threads so tight,
Taught her to soften, to seek the light.
Not weak to feel, nor wrong to know,
But strength in learning when to let go.

She learned that pain did not define,
That healing is a steady climb.
Through self-compassion, she reclaimed her space,
No longer a shadow, but full of grace.

She let her heart and mind embrace,
No longer locked in their endless chase.
Logic gave wisdom; emotion gave light,
Together, they formed a soul burning bright.

She found love, not in their words,
But in the song, her own heart heard.
She gave herself the joy once sought,
Validated by the life she fought.

No longer torn, no longer small,

She stood with pride. She had it all.

Forgiving the past, embracing her name,

Dominique, never lost, never the same.

She once felt unseen, a love denied,

But grace had held her all the while.

Not by chance, nor cast aside,

She was chosen, cherished, divine.

Interactive Reflection: The Inner Weather Report

At the end of each day this week, pause and ask yourself: What is my inner weather today?

You might write: "Cloudy with frustration." Or, "Clear skies, light breeze of joy."

Then, reflect:

- What contributed to this weather?

- What did I do that helped regulate or shift it?

Emotional self-awareness is like forecasting. The more you track, the better you get at preparing. Your weather may change, but your anchor remains within.

Chapter 10
Building a Stronger You: Words, Strategy, and Action

"I've seen the mind endure war, heartbreak, and loss. But I've also seen it rebuild, with words as bricks and hope as mortar."

- Dr. C. A. Castillo

This final chapter of The Resilient Mind: Harnessing Inner Strength to Guide the Body is more than a reflection; it's a call to action. The insights throughout this book have laid the foundation, but fundamental transformation begins when we apply them. This chapter equips you with the mindset, strategies, and tools to take ownership of your life, harness your inner strength, and move forward with purpose. It is the bridge between understanding resilience and fully embodying it.

The Power of Words: Building Resilience from the Inside Out

Words shape our reality in profound ways. More than just speech, the words we use, especially in our internal dialogue, become the lens through which we view ourselves and the world. They either build us up or quietly break us down.

Negative self-talk breeds doubt and weakens resilience. On the other hand, choosing empowering language nurtures mental strength, enabling us to face challenges with clarity and composure. To develop resilience, we must consciously use language that affirms our growth, capacity, and worth.

This is also where SMART goals come into play. A resilient mind plans strategically. The SMART framework Specific, Measurable, Achievable, Relevant, and Time-bound and transforms vague intentions into actionable steps. It's easier to maintain momentum when your goals are clear and achievable. Through strategic goal setting, we regain a sense of control and direction, no longer drifting but progressing with intention.

Words guide our thoughts, and goals drive our actions. Together, they form the cornerstone of mental resilience. But to sustain this balance, we also need emotional regulation and the ability to pause before reacting. This brings us to the balloon and snake analogies.

Slowing Down: The Balloon and the Snake

Resilience isn't about suppressing emotions; it's about managing them. The snake analogy teaches us that a baby snake, unable to regulate its instincts, releases all its venom when threatened. This reflects how unfiltered emotional reactions often lead to damage both to ourselves and others.

Similarly, think of a balloon: the more air you force into it, the closer it comes to bursting. This mirrors how suppressed emotions if left unaddressed, can erupt in destructive ways. Emotional energy, if not consciously regulated, builds pressure until it spills out, sometimes with painful consequences.

Learning to pause creates space for awareness. It allows us to choose a response rather than default to a reaction. This pause, this breath, is where resilience is built. Healthy emotional release isn't passive. It might look like taking time out, journaling, walking in nature, or speaking to someone you trust.

These intentional pauses allow emotions to settle and clarity to emerge. The goal isn't to avoid feeling; it's to feel wise. While some of our emotional responses are shaped by genetics or upbringing, resilience is not fixed. It's something we can strengthen. This brings us to the nature versus nurture discussion.

Nature, Nurture, and Forgiveness: Letting Go to Grow

Resilience is both innate and grown. While we may inherit certain tendencies, our capacity to grow through hardship is primarily influenced by the choices we make and the practices we commit to. One of the most powerful tools for growth is forgiveness, not for others, but for ourselves.

Forgiveness is often misunderstood. It isn't about excusing wrongdoing; it's about releasing yourself from the weight of what no longer serves you. Holding onto anger or resentment is like carrying a bag of waste, unnecessary and increasingly harmful. The longer we cling to it, the more it festers. Forgiveness allows us to set that weight down, freeing up energy that can be redirected toward healing, growth, and peace.

This also includes forgiving ourselves, acknowledging past missteps, learning from them, and choosing to move forward. It's an act of courage and self-compassion.

To forgive is also to make space to identify what no longer aligns with your values. This leads us to the idea of incongruence, living a life that reflects others' expectations rather than your own truth.

When your external life doesn't match your inner truth, it creates dissonance, restlessness, and dissatisfaction. Letting go of incongruence is essential for authentic resilience. Like a snake sheds its skin, we must shed outdated beliefs, habits, and identities to make room for who we are becoming.

Forgiveness: Letting Go for Yourself

Forgiveness is a powerful act not for the person being forgiven but for the one doing the forgiving. Too often, we carry the weight of past hurt, clinging to anger as though it serves justice. In truth, holding onto resentment only binds us emotionally to what we're trying to move past.

Resilience begins with healing, and healing requires forgiveness not as a gift to others but as a release for ourselves. Letting go of grudges allows our minds and bodies to release stored tension, making room for growth and renewal. Forgiveness is essential for self-healing. It frees us from the toxic grip of bitterness and opens the door to emotional liberation. When we let go of the past, we reclaim our peace and our power. We stop letting old wounds dictate our future. In doing so, we build emotional resilience, focusing not on what hurts us but on what's possible ahead.

Forgiving doesn't mean forgetting or excusing pain. It means choosing not to be chained to it. This emotional release helps us take back control so that we can move forward with strength. Forgiveness teaches us emotional responsibility: the ability to choose peace over pain and clarity over chaos.

Jettison: The Art of Letting Go

Letting go, also known as jettisoning, is the intentional practice of releasing emotional baggage, outdated beliefs, and unhealthy attachments that weigh us down. To build emotional resilience, we must learn to recognize when something no longer serves our well-being. Holding onto old grudges, toxic relationships, or destructive thought patterns only blocks personal growth and traps us in emotional stagnation. Jettisoning lightens our emotional load, making room for new, healthier experiences and perspectives.

Just as a ship must discard excess weight to navigate rough waters, we, too, must release unnecessary burdens to move through life with clarity and purpose. Letting go isn't about shirking responsibility, it's about discerning what is essential and what no longer belongs. This requires courage: the bravery to face discomfort, to make difficult decisions, and to trust that release is a necessary part of resilience. When we let go of what holds us back, we create a life that feels more spacious, intentional, and fulfilling.

Letting go also shapes how we view relationships. People come into our lives for a reason, a season, or a lifetime, and recognizing this truth helps us release attachments to those who may no longer align with our growth. Some are meant to teach us something; others accompany us for a while; a few will walk the journey with us long-term. Embracing this reality empowers us to focus on relationships that nourish us rather than clinging to those that no longer serve our emotional well-being. It's an emotional shedding that makes space for transformation.

People Come into Your Life for a Reason, a Season, or a Lifetime

Understanding the role different individuals play in our lives is essential for emotional clarity and growth. Some relationships arrive to teach us lessons. Others are companions for a chapter. A rare few are meant to stay for the long haul. Embracing this perspective allows us to appreciate the value of each connection without becoming overly attached.

Just like the seasons, relationships evolve. The key to emotional resilience lies in discerning when to nurture a connection and when to let go. Some relationships challenge us; others comfort us. But all of them, whether temporary or lasting, help shape who we are.

By honoring the natural flow of human connection, we create room for peace and personal growth. In learning this, we begin to recognize the importance of releasing outdated beliefs and clinging patterns. We begin shedding the emotional layers that no longer serve us, just like a snake sheds its old skin to grow.

Shedding the Old Skin: The Snake Analogy for Growth

The snake analogy offers a powerful reminder that transformation demands release. Just as a snake must shed its old skin to thrive, we must let go of outdated beliefs, limiting thoughts, and emotional habits that no longer serve our growth. Holding on to the past only blocks us from becoming who we are meant to be.

Shedding old skin is not always comfortable. In fact, it's often painful. But it's through this process of discomfort that true growth emerges. Emotional resilience is built through these moments of shedding when we face uncertainty, confront fear, and choose evolution over stagnation. Remaining in old patterns is merely surviving. Letting go, on the other hand, opens the door to truly living. It's how we move forward one layer at a time toward becoming who we truly are.

Being Alive vs. Truly Living

There's a difference between existing and living. Being alive means breathing, functioning, and moving through the motions. Genuinely living, however, is a choice. It means showing up, engaging with life meaningfully, and aligning our actions with our values.

To live fully is to meet life with presence, curiosity, and courage. A resilient mind doesn't just get by, it thrives. It makes intentional choices, seeks growth, and nurtures joy. This shift from mere survival to purposeful living is what resilience is really about.

Authentic living requires awareness of both the mind and heart. It's the conscious pursuit of meaning, joy, and authenticity. In this space, we step into our power, guided not just by goals but by Wisdom and purpose.

The Dom Family: Kingdom, Wisdom, and Freedom

The Dom Family kingdom, Wisdom, and Freedom represent the pillars of resilient living. Kingdom is about owning your inner authority: taking responsibility for your life. Wisdom is the insight gained through life's trials and triumphs. Freedom is the liberation that comes from living in alignment with your truth.

Together, these principles form a foundation for inner strength. Kingdom reminds us we are the authors of our story. Wisdom equips us with the tools to navigate life's challenges. Freedom unchains us from fear and shame, allowing us to move forward with courage and grace.

When we embody these principles, we shift from reactive to intentional. Life becomes less about controlling outcomes and more about honoring the process. We begin to enjoy the journey, not just endure it, trusting that each step is part of a meaningful unfolding.

Strength Through Adversity: Pressure Creates Diamonds

Adversity is an inevitable part of life. It may feel overwhelming, but it's often in these moments that our true strength emerges. The metaphor of pressure-creating diamonds reminds us that challenge is not the end; it's a refining force that shapes us.

Just as carbon under pressure becomes a diamond, our hardships can become the foundation of our most excellent resilience. The key is to harness that pressure, not be crushed by it. When we confront difficulties head-on, we grow, adapt, and build a more durable sense of self.

Strength through adversity doesn't mean the struggle is painless, it means we rise anyway. Each time we overcome a challenge, our mental endurance grows. A resilient mind sees pain as part of the journey and uses it as fuel to move forward.

Adversity also teaches us to carry only what belongs to us. Many suffer under the weight of others' emotions, taking on burdens they were never meant to bear. But resilience involves discernment, knowing what it's ours to carry, and setting boundaries around the rest.

Carrying Burdens That Aren't Yours: Self-Care and Boundaries

Boundaries and self-care are essential to emotional well-being, yet many struggle with the guilt of saying no. When we constantly carry the emotional loads of others, we drain ourselves and risk burning out. To foster resilience, we must protect our mental and emotional space.

Boundaries aren't walls; they are doorways that allow healthy interaction while honoring your limits. Setting them is an act of love, not rejection. It ensures you have enough energy for your challenges and prevents resentment from building.

Protecting your energy starts with knowing your limits and being intentional about how you spend your emotional resources. A resilient mind prioritizes self-care, recognizing that rest and recovery are just as important as action. Without these, our minds become overwhelmed, and our bodies suffer.

Sustainable growth requires patience. There's often pressure to "fix" everything at once, but resilience begins right where you are. Small, consistent steps create lasting change. Establishing boundaries and tending to your well-being is how you gain the strength to move forward mindfully and intentionally.

Start Where You Are: The Power of Beginning Now

Many people feel stuck, waiting for the "perfect" moment to change. But the truth is, the best place to begin is exactly where you are. Resilience starts with presence, not perfection.

Progress doesn't come from dreaming of the destination. It comes from taking grounded, consistent steps in the present. Acknowledge your starting point. Accept your current reality. Then, choose to move forward, one step at a time.

This mindset is especially vital when it comes to emotional expression. Society often teaches boys to suppress vulnerability, equating crying with weakness. But emotional expression is a strength, not a flaw.

Crying is a natural release of emotion. Teaching boys that it's okay to feel and express themselves builds mental and emotional resilience. It nurtures emotional intelligence and helps them respond to life's challenges with openness and balance. By embracing where you are, you permit yourself to grow. Resilience isn't about denying your pain or pretending to be strong, it's about honoring your experience and choosing to rise from it.

Protecting Your Energy: Starting from the Inside Out

Resilience is an inside-out process. It begins with protecting one's energy from distractions and demands that don't serve one's growth. By setting clear emotional boundaries, one conserves energy for what truly matters.

This protection is rooted in alignment, knowing your values, and acting in ways that reflect them. When we live in alignment, we become more grounded and intentional. We stop leaking energy into situations that don't deserve it.

A resilient mind knows when to pause, when to say no, and when to walk away. Boundaries aren't selfish, they are essential. They keep us grounded, clear-headed, and capable of showing up fully in our lives.

Letting go of vengeance is another form of energy protection. The desire for revenge drains us. Forgiveness through difficulty is liberating. It breaks the cycle of pain and allows peace to return. True resilience is not only about enduring hardship. It's about rising above it with grace, clarity, and the power to choose peace over conflict.

Would You Rather Be Right or Happy?

Often, we find ourselves locked in the pursuit of being right, proving a point, winning an argument, or defending our stance. But what if happiness matters more? Choosing happiness over being right requires humility. It means releasing the need for control and prioritizing connection over ego. A resilient mind understands that being right isn't always worth the emotional cost.

When we cling to being right, we often create division. But when we choose peace, we invite harmony. We begin to value understanding over winning and empathy over validation. This choice between being right and happy reflects what we truly value.

Happiness is a form of wisdom. It's the quiet strength that chooses peace over pride. Sometimes, the greatest act of strength is letting go, not because we lose, but because we choose what truly matters.

Enjoying the Journey Instead of Being Distracted by the Destination

In today's fast-paced world, it's easy to become fixated on the destination, whether that's a specific goal, a milestone, or the next significant achievement. We often link our sense of fulfillment to reaching that endpoint, but this mindset can rob us of joy in the present. When we measure success only by what lies ahead, we risk missing the meaning and beauty found in the journey itself.

True resilience begins when we learn to embrace the process. Every experience we gather along the way, whether triumphant or challenging, shapes us. When we shift our focus from the end goal to the steps we take to get there, we open ourselves to deeper fulfillment, personal growth, and a more grounded sense of purpose.

Enjoying the journey means finding value in the process: the lessons learned, the growth earned, and the quiet victories we might otherwise overlook. Each moment, however small, contributes to who we are becoming. This mindset nurtures gratitude, presence, and emotional awareness. Rather than rushing ahead, we learn to pause, reflect, and celebrate progress in real time.

This philosophy aligns with the core principles of Kingdom, Wisdom, and Freedom. The Kingdom represents the strength of our inner world, grounding us in the present. Wisdom invites us to learn from each experience with clarity and humility. Freedom gives us the space to enjoy the process, free from the pressure of performance or outcome. Resilience, then, isn't just about reaching the destination it's about being transformed by the journey. The more we lean into the ride, the more we grow, and the more meaningful our path becomes.

Incongruence: Living a Life That Isn't Yours

Many people live lives shaped not by their desires but by the expectations of others, parents, society, culture, or fear of letting someone down. This disconnect between one's true self and the life they lead is called incongruence. It creates inner tension, emotional fatigue, and a quiet sense of loss.

Imagine a young man whose parents insisted he become a doctor, even though his heart was in music. He complies, excels in school, and eventually becomes a respected physician. On the outside, he appears successful. But inside, he feels numb, distant from himself. Each day, he wakes up to a life that doesn't reflect his truth. That's incongruence: when your external reality clashes with your internal values.

It's important to note that incongruence isn't the same as temporary discomfort. Growth often requires us to push through fear and self-doubt to reach meaningful goals. However, accurate alignment comes when we pursue a life that genuinely reflects who we are, not one built around obligation or pretense.

This concept connects directly with the message of The Resilient Mind: Harnessing Inner Strength to Guide the Body. On the book cover, the Phoenix represents resilience, the rebirth that comes after struggle. The tear symbolizes healing, acknowledging pain without being defined by it. From that tear, a body of water forms, and a brain rises, signifying how healing brings clarity, strength, and renewal to the mind.

Like the Phoenix, we must let go of what no longer serves us: expectations, fear, and incongruence so we can rise. Only when our minds and hearts are aligned can we live with authenticity and freedom. So, ask yourself: Are you living a life that truly belongs to you? Or are you surviving in a story that someone else wrote?

Ikigai: The Reason for Being

At the heart of a resilient life is the ability to find meaning and purpose. This is where the Japanese concept of Ikigai comes in. Ikigai is the intersection of four essential elements: what you love, what you're good at, what the world needs, and what you can be paid for. When these align, life flows with purpose. You no longer just exist, you thrive.

Those who discover their Ikigai wake each day with a sense of direction. They know their work matters and their actions are tied to something greater than themselves. Unlike a life driven by survival or performance, Ikigai offers lasting fulfillment and emotional well-being. Many people struggle to find this balance because they've been conditioned to chase external validation such as money, titles, and approval. This can create deep incongruence, leaving them feeling disconnected from their passions and exhausted by a life that looks good but feels wrong.

Resilience requires us to strip away external pressures and return to what truly matters. Like the Phoenix, we must honor our past struggles, shed what's inauthentic, and rise renewed. Once again, the Phoenix's tear represents this healing. From that tear, the mind emerges clear, focused, and free. So, as you close this chapter and this book, ask yourself:

- Are you living in alignment with your Ikigai, or are you moving through life on autopilot?

- What small change can you make today that brings you closer to a life of purpose, passion, and presence?

This is not the end. It is the beginning of your journey toward deeper alignment. When the mind is strong, it will always lead the body home.

Interactive Reflection: Your Personal Resilience Plan

You've traveled far in this book, and now it's time to carry your tools into daily life.

Answer the following in your journal:

- What's one emotional area I want to grow in right now?

- Which tools from this book will I commit to using in the next 30 days?

- Who can I invite to walk with me in this — a friend, a therapist, a coach?

Resilience isn't a destination. It's a way of showing up, again and again, with intention, integrity, and hope.

Conclusion

"This is not the end; it is the beginning of you becoming whole. You have always had the power. Now, you have the awareness to use it."

— Dr. C. A. Castillo

The Resilient Mind: Harnessing Inner Strength to Guide the Body

As we reach the end of The Resilient Mind: Harnessing Inner Strength to Guide the Body, it's important to remember that resilience isn't a fixed destination, it's an ongoing journey. The tools, strategies, and insights shared throughout this book aren't meant to lead you to perfection but to guide you toward a more grounded, balanced, and empowered life. By developing emotional resilience and inner strength, we give ourselves the ability to face life's challenges, whether large or small, with grace, intention, and clarity.

Throughout this journey, we've explored many dimensions of resilience, from the power of words and the value of strategic tools like SMART goals and SWOT analysis to the healing practices of forgiveness, emotional expression, and self-care. We've uncovered the importance of shedding old patterns, grieving what was lost, and making space for something new. And we've discovered that adversity isn't a dead end, it's the fire through which we are shaped. Just like a diamond form under pressure, so can our greatest strength emerge from life's most challenging moments.

As you move forward, remember that resilience is about more than surviving; it's about thriving. It's about choosing to live fully, embracing each step of the journey with openness and courage. Every day is a new opportunity to align your mind and body in harmony. You have the power to choose how you respond to life's inevitable ups and downs. Will you fixate on the destination, or will you embrace the beauty of the process and the wisdom it brings?

The choice is yours.

As you continue to harness your inner strength, you may find freedom, insight, and fulfillment in every moment. Keep building the resilient mind that guides your path, empowering you to create and live the life you truly desire. And remember, it's not about how you start; it's about how you finish.

This book was written for those who feel like they don't belong, for those who've been handed a difficult deck in life. If that's you, I hope this journey has offered even a flicker of hope. May it inspire you to take back the reigns of your mind and, in doing so, guide your body toward healing, balance, and purpose.

Contact Information:

drcastillo@mrc5.com

cacastillo@cltsolution.com

Appendix

Examples of Levels of Emotion / Feelings Chart

Emotion	Level One (High)	Level Two (Medium)	Level Three (Low)
Anger	Embittered Disgruntled Sore	Irritated Bothered Exasperated	Irked, Disheartened
Depression	Sad Despair Hopeless	Awful Dispirited Tearful.	Temperamental Somber Bleak
Hurt	Persecuted, Abused, Maltreated	Belittled, Devalued, Wounded	Minimized Put Down Neglected
Happy	Elated Euphoric Thrilled	Cheerful Merry Elated	Contented Genial Sunny
Fear	Distressed, Petrified, Frightened	Afraid Scared, Threatened	Cautious Tense Worried

Understanding Emotional Levels

Emotions operate on different levels, and recognizing the appropriate level is key to responding effectively. Any given emotion generally has three levels. Accurately identifying where your emotion falls can help you process and manage it better.

For instance, someone might say they feel a strong, high-intensity emotion on the anger spectrum (Level 1). However, upon reflection, they might actually feel bothered by a milder form of anger (Level 2). Addressing the emotion of being bothered instead of embittered can lead to more productive emotional work and healing.

A more comprehensive list of emotional levels can help you identify where you stand. To explore this in greater depth, consider working with a licensed mental health clinician who can help you understand how these emotional levels work and how to navigate them.

TEA Method (Part 1): Triggers, Emotions, Actions

This is a technique I developed to help individuals better understand and respond to their emotional experiences.

T = Trigger | E = Emotion | A = Action

For every trigger, there is an emotion. And for every emotion, there is an action. The goal is to begin identifying your triggers. A trigger can be a person, place, or thing that evokes an emotional response.

Once a trigger is recognized, the next step is to pinpoint the emotion it provokes. Then, observe the action you typically take in response to that emotion. If that action tends to be harmful or unproductive, you have the power to choose a healthier, more constructive alternative.

This process encourages emotional awareness and intentional behavior change, creating a more empowered and mindful way of living.

Trigger	Remembering a person who is not around on their birthday
Emotion	Depress
Action	Cry

Trigger	Seeing a picture of a place where you visited
Emotion	Happy
Action	Smile

Trigger	Looking at someone who looks like a person who did something bad to you
Emotion	Angry
Action	Punching that person in the face

Trigger	Thinking about paying a bill that is coming due
Emotion	Anxious
Action	Drink alcohol

Trigger	Hearing someone yelling at a child
Emotion	Fear
Action	Start shaking and sweating

Trigger	Hearing a song that reminds you of a loved one who has passed
Emotion	Grief
Action	Start screaming, "Why did you leave? I need you."

Trigger	Watching a scene in a movie that made you feel bad that you didn't act
Emotion	Guilt
Action	Allow someone to treat you like crap

Trigger(s), Emotion (s), Action(s) React or Respond = TEAR (Part 2)

The second part of this technique is to practice alternate actions if the first action is negative. By identifying the triggers that lead to an emotion that then leads to an alternative action, the person can learn to respond (positive) instead of reacting (negative). For the most part, the reaction usually has instant gratification but long-term consequences, whereas responding usually does not lead to instant gratification but long-term success.

Trigger	Remembering a person who is not around on their birthday
Emotion	Depress
Action	Cry
Alternate Action	Exercise

Trigger	Seeing a picture of a place where someone visited
Emotion	Happy
Action	Smile
Alternate Action	No need for alternate action

Trigger	Looking at someone who looks like a person who did something bad to you
Emotion	Angry
Action	Punching that person in the face
Alternate Action	Thinking about punching the person, instead, go for a walk

Trigger	Thinking about paying a bill that is coming due
Emotion	Anxious
Action	Drink alcohol
Alternate Action	Pray

Trigger	Hearing someone yelling at a child
Emotion	Fear
Action	Start shaking and sweating
Alternate Action	Talking to someone or a therapist

Trigger	Hearing a song that reminds you of a loved one who has passed
Emotion	Grief
Action	Start screaming, "Why did you leave? I need you."

Alternate Action	Smiling, remembering a good memory

Trigger	Watching a scene in a movie made you feel bad that you didn't act.
Emotion	Guilt
Action	Allow someone to treat you like crap
Alternate Action	Forgive self

I would like for the readers of this book to practice this exercise called the TEA Test to learn how to identify your TEA and change your actions so they will be positive.

TEA | TEAR2

Below is a blank example that you can use to practice this exercise for yourself. Please remember this does not replace seeking proper mental health. This is just a tool that can be used to help learn triggers.

Trigger	
Emotion	
Action	

Trigger	
Emotion	
Action	
Alternate Action	

Self-Compassion

Self	Love
Self	Understanding
Self	Forgiveness
Self	Kindness
Self	Patience

Understand	Love
Understand	Self
Understand	Forgiveness
Understand	Kindness
Understand	Patience

Once you learn self-compassion, you will have compassion for others. I believe that only through self-compassion can someone really have compassion for someone else. Imagine how the world could be if we all learn and practice self-compassion.

Self-Validation

Validation is acknowledgment. Some people are stuck because they seek validation from someone who may never give to them or cannot give to them. Once you learn self-validation, there is no need to get it from others. You may want it, but it will not be necessary. If you get it, it can just be like icing on the cake.

Five Things

Can't Change	Can Change
Biological Parents	Parents
People	Yourself/Mindset
Death is Guaranteed	Friends
Past	Environment
Birthday	Clothes

Serenity Prayer

God Grant me the Serenity to Accept the things I cannot change, the courage to change the things I can, and the wisdom to know the difference.

This exercise is called Can't vs. Can. In this exercise, you come up with five things that you, me, or anyone in the world cannot change, no matter how hard we try. Then, come up with five things that you can change.

Out of the two categories, category one being what we can't change and category two is what we can change, which category was the easiest to come up with? If it is category one that was the hardest, that could be where depression, anxiety, anger, guilt, grief, or fear is born.

Could you imagine if you put effort towards the things you can change instead of the things you cannot? Life may be more manageable. This should be the focus. And remember, no one is perfect, and we all make mistakes; therefore, stop putting energy towards things you cannot change and put it towards things you can. This can help with your mindset.

A. Cognitive Behavioral Tools for Building Resilience

1. Thought Record Chart

- o This tool helps individuals identify negative thoughts and replace them with more balanced, positive alternatives.

- o **Purpose:** To challenge negative thinking patterns and cultivate a healthier, more resilient mindset.

Date/Time	Situation	Automatic Thoughts	Alternative Thoughts	Outcome

2. ABC Model Chart

- **A (Activating Event):** Identify the event or situation that triggered the emotional response.

- **B (Belief):** Examine the belief or thought that led to the emotional response.

- **C (Consequence):** Describe the emotional or behavioral consequence of the belief.

- **Purpose:** This tool helps individuals understand the connection between their thoughts, emotions, and behaviors.

A (Activating Event)	B (Belief)	C (Consequences)	Alternative Belief	New Outcome

B. Mindfulness Exercises for Emotional Regulation

1. **Body Scan Meditation Chart**

   o This exercise encourages individuals to focus on each part of their body to increase awareness and reduce stress.

   o **Purpose:** To promote relaxation and mindfulness through attention to physical sensations.

Body Area	Sensation Felt	Duration (Minutes)
Head		
Shoulder		
Chest		
Hands/Arms		
Legs/Feet		

2. Grounding Exercise Chart

- This tool guides individuals through the process of grounding themselves by connecting to their physical surroundings.

- **Purpose:** To reduce anxiety and bring awareness to the present moment.

Step	What to Focus On	Duration (minutes)
Look Around	Identify five things you see	
Touch	Identify four things you feel	
Listen	Identify three things you hear	
Smell	Identify two things you smell	
Taste	Identify one thing you taste	

What are 5 things you can see? Look for small details such as a pattern on the ceiling, the way light reflects off a surface, or an object you never noticed.

What are 4 things you can feel? Notice the sensation of clothing on your body, the sun on your skin, or the feeling of the chair you are sitting in. Pick up an object and examine its weight, texture, and other physical qualities.

What are 3 things you can hear? Pay special attention to the sounds your mind has tuned out, such as a ticking clock, distant traffic, or trees blowing in the wind.

What are 2 things you can smell? Try to notice smells in the air around you, like an air freshener or freshly mowed grass. You may also look around for something that has a scent, such as a flower or an unlit candle.

What is 1 thing you can taste? Carry gum, candy, or small snacks for this step. Pop one in your mouth and focus your attention closely on the flavors.

Date	Today's Challenge	What did I learn from it	What can I do differently tomorrow

C. Journaling Prompts for Self-Reflection and Growth

1. **Daily Resilience Journal**
   - o A tool to help individuals reflect on their daily experiences, challenges, and triumphs in building resilience.

2. Gratitude Journal

- A tool for cultivating a mindset of gratitude by encouraging individuals to write down three things they are grateful for each day.

Date	What I'm Grateful for Today

D. Self-Compassion Exercises

1. Self-Compassion Letter

- o This exercise encourages individuals to write a compassionate letter to themselves, especially when feeling upset or critical.

- o **Purpose:** To foster self-kindness and break patterns of self-criticism.

Situation	How I feel	Self-Compassion

IKIGAI Diagram

Recommended Reading

1. Hurt People, Hurt People *by Dr. Sandra Wilson*

A powerful exploration of how unresolved pain from the past can affect current relationships and behaviors. This book helped me understand the importance of healing and self-awareness in breaking negative cycles.

2. Rich Dad, Poor Dad *by Robert Kiyosaki*

A groundbreaking perspective on financial education, this book shifted the way I view money, investments, and the mindset necessary for financial success.

3. Think and Grow Rich *by Napoleon Hill*

It is one of the most impactful books on the psychology of wealth. It taught me that success is not just about hard work but also about the mindset and determination to achieve my goals.

4. Interview with the Devil *by Napoleon Hill*

An intriguing narrative on overcoming inner demons and understanding the forces that hold us back. Hill's take on fear and self-sabotage really resonated with me.

5. Start with Why *by Simon Sinek*

Sinek's approach to leadership and motivation emphasizes the power of purpose. It inspired me to focus on my "why" in everything I do, both personally and professionally.

6. The Millionaire Next Door *by Thomas J. Stanley and William D. Danko*

A look at the habits and lifestyles of self-made millionaires. This book provided valuable insights into the discipline, frugality, and long-term planning necessary for financial success.

7. Breaking the Psychological Chain of Slavery *by Dr. Welsing*

A thought-provoking read on the psychological effects of slavery and how it has impacted communities. This book reinforced the importance of understanding our collective history in order to heal and move forward.

8. **Atomic Habits** *by James Clear*

A must-read for anyone looking to build lasting change in their lives. Clear's practical advice on how to create small habits that lead to big results helped me understand the power of incremental growth.

9. **Machiavelli** *(The Prince)*

An essential work on political philosophy and power dynamics. This book sharpened my understanding of strategy, leadership, and the often harsh realities of governance.

10. **The Art of Seduction** *by Robert Greene*

A controversial yet insightful look at the psychology of influence and attraction. Greene's exploration of power dynamics was both fascinating and enlightening.

11. **Making it to the Top: Lessons from a Service Member** *by Dr. C. A. Castillo*

A powerful reflection on discipline, leadership, and perseverance from a military perspective. This book connected deeply with my own service experience, reinforcing the values of resilience, honor, and purpose.

12. **Valuable Assets Lead Us to Excellence and Success (VALUES)** *by Dr. C. A. Castillo*

An inspiring guide on turning core values into success principles. It reminded me how essential it is to remain grounded in integrity and character while striving for excellence.

13. **Lessons from My Dad: Life, Finance, Credit, and Investments by** *Malique D. Castillo and Dr. C. A. Castillo*

A heartfelt and practical book filled with generational wisdom on navigating life and money. It reminded me of the importance of legacy, family, and teaching through example.

14. **The Let Them Theory by** *Mel Robbins*

In line with The Resilient Mind, Mel Robbins "Let them Theory teaches the power of letting go of control and focusing on your own peace. By allowing others to be who they are, you conserve your energy and build inner strength through acceptance and self-trust.

15. How to Let Things Go by *Shunmyo Masuno*

This Zen-inspired guide complements The Resilient Mind by showing how simplicity and mindfulness can help release emotional burdens. Masuno's teaching promotes resilience by encouraging clarity, calm, and presence in everyday life.

www.ingramcontent.com/pod-product-compliance
Lightning Source LLC
Chambersburg PA
CBHW071241130626
46556CB00003B/1111